Summer Solutions.

Minutes a Day-Mastery for a Lifetime!

Level 5

Study Skills

Nancy Tondy

Bright Ideas Press, LLC
Cleveland, OH

Summer Solutions Level 5
Study Skills

Printed in the United States of America

ISBN: 978-1-60873-141-1

Cover Design: Dan Mazzola
Editors: Kimberly A. Dambrogio
Thomas P. Bucco
Illustrator: Christopher Backs

Instructions for Parents / Guardians

- *Summer Solutions* is an extension of the *Simple Solutions* Approach being used by thousands of children in schools across the United States.
- The 30 lessons included in each workbook are meant to review and reinforce the skills learned in the grade level just completed.
- The program is designed to be used three days per week for ten weeks to ensure retention.
- Completing the book all at one time defeats the purpose of sustained practice over the summer break.
- Each book contains answers for each lesson.
- Each book also contains Help Pages, which list vocabulary, test-taking and study strategies, references, and other helpful information.
- Lessons should be checked immediately for optimal feedback.
- Adjust the use of the book to fit vacations. More lessons may have to be completed during the weeks before or following a family vacation.

Summer Solutions Level 5 Study Skills

Table of Contents

Topic	Page
Main Idea	2
Analogies	4
Summarizing	6
Context Clues	8
Cause and Effect	10
Fact and Opinion	14
Using Mnemonic Devices	16
Other Memory Strategies	18
Graphic Organizers: Tables and Charts	22
Graphic Organizers: Three-Column Charts and Venn Diagrams	24
Graphic Organizers: Timelines	26
Graphic Organizers: Graphs	28 – 31
Diagrams	32
Test-Taking Strategies and Tips	36
Essay Writing	38
Parts of a Textbook	41
Using Resources	42
Avoiding Plagiarism	44
Creating a Bibliography	46

Summer Solutions Level 5
Study Skills

Reviewed Skills Include

- Finding and Paraphrasing the Main Idea
- Solving Analogies
- Using Context Clues
- Working with Graphic Organizers
- Interpreting Graphs, Diagrams, and Timelines
- Using Mnemonics
- Taking Effective Notes
- Enhancing Test-Taking Skills
- Developing Research Strategies
- Avoiding Plagiarism

Help Pages begin on page 63.

Answers to Lessons begin on page 83.

Lesson #1

Main Idea

The **main idea** is what a paragraph or selection is mostly about. Usually, there is just one main idea, and you can sometimes find it in a **topic sentence**. A topic sentence can be anywhere within a paragraph or passage. In a well-written passage, all sentences support the main idea. To find the main idea, ask, "What is this writing mostly about?"

1. Underline the sentence that gives the definition of **main idea.**

2. To find the main idea, ask yourself, "____

   ____?"

3. How many main ideas are there in a well-written passage? ______________

During the 1800s, people traveled three ways: by walking, by riding on horseback, or by riding in horse-drawn wagons. Instead of paved roads, there were only muddy paths that had been built on Indian trails. Sometimes boats were available, but they were very slow. Travel was not only difficult, it could be very dangerous, and most people did not travel because of this. Some people never traveled away from the place where they were born.

4. What is the main idea of the paragraph above?

   A) Before the invention of cars and airplanes, people only traveled in wagons or boats.

   B) Years ago, people relied mostly on horses for transportation.

   C) During the 1800s, travel was difficult and dangerous, so most people did not travel.

   D) Compared to today, travel was very difficult during the 1800s.

5. Highlight four different types of transportation noted in the paragraph. If you do not have a highlighter, underline the words with a pen or pencil.

6. **Synonyms are words that have the same or nearly the same meaning.** Which two words are synonyms? Use a dictionary if you are not sure.

   dangerous   courageous   ingenious   hazardous

Each set of sentences below can make a paragraph. Read all the sentences in each set, and decide which sentence is the topic sentence.

7. A) Nicholas has $15 dollars to spend.
   B) He can buy movie tickets for himself and a friend, or he can buy a used video game at the resale shop.
   C) The movie will last for two hours, but the video game will last much longer.
   D) As a consumer, Nicholas must decide which choice provides the greatest benefit for a cost of $15.

8. A) After the voyages of Christopher Columbus, two French men went to North America to search for a trade route.
   B) Jacques Cartier explored the St. Lawrence River in 1535.
   C) In 1608, Samuel de Champlain looked for a trade route through North America.
   D) Cartier helped France colonize what is now Canada.
   E) Champlain set up a fur-trading post in what is now the city of Quebec.

Study Strategy

Develop your own highlighting system. Use one color for marking the main idea and another color for marking new vocabulary and definitions. Don't use too many colors; that can be confusing.

Lesson #2

Analogies

An **analogy** compares two sets of words or objects that are alike in some way. Synonym analogies compare synonyms, like this:

happy : cheerful :: easy : effortless

(You say, "Happy is to cheerful as easy is to effortless.")

Both sides of the analogy are related in the same way. In this example, they are synonyms. Here is another type of analogy:

breakfast : morning :: lunch : noontime

(You say, "Breakfast is to morning as lunch is to noontime.")

Breakfast is the meal of the morning, and lunch is the meal of noontime. Analogies compare many different kinds of things. Besides synonym analogies, there are antonym analogies, description analogies, and part-to-whole analogies. (See the *Help Pages* for more examples of analogies.) To solve an analogy, you need to figure out what the relationship is between the set of words that is given. Try these:

1. In this analogy, what is the **relationship** between the first two words?

   peach : fruit :: corn : _______

   A) The first word is a synonym or antonym of the second word.
   B) The second word names a group; the first word is a member of it.

2. Which word completes the analogy? peach : fruit :: corn : _______

   grow crop yellow vegetable

Choose the word that best completes each analogy.

3. boat : sail :: ________ : fly

   house sink helicopter atmosphere

4. mouse : furry :: porcupine : ____________

prickly forest outdoors trap

5. intelligent : ________ :: idea : thought

believe clever school books

Read the paragraph and then complete the items that follow.

There are many different shapes, sizes, and types of rivers. A **subterranean** river is a type of river that flows underground or through a cave. Subterranean rivers may form through chemical weathering, a process that takes millions of years. These rivers are home to certain animals, which have adapted to the dark conditions of the underground. This adaptation also took many, many years.

6. What is the main idea of the paragraph? Fill in the circle completely.

- ◯ A subterranean river is a certain type of river with its own characteristics.
- ◯ Subterranean rivers can be found all over the world.
- ◯ Rivers consist of fresh water, and oceans consist of salt water.
- ◯ Subterranean rivers are hidden and mysterious.

7. Which of these sentences best supports the main idea of the paragraph?

A) Sometimes a river is smaller than a creek.
B) Rivers, lakes, and oceans are important parts of the water cycle.
C) The name comes from two Latin roots; sub means "under," and terra means "Earth."
D) Often, an underground river will be featured in a myth or adventure story.

8. In a well-written passage, all sentences support the

____.

Lesson #3

Summarizing

Once you have practiced finding the main idea, you will be able to summarize information. When you **summarize** or **paraphrase**, you use your own words. A summary includes the main ideas and some of the supporting details of a selection but not all the extra information. Follow the steps below for summarizing:

- Read all of the information in the selection.
- Highlight some of the key points or jot them down on paper as you are reading. If you are taking notes for a report, be sure to write the title and the author's name; you will need this later.
- Begin your summary by explaining the main points. Use your own words to tell what the selection is mostly about.
- Add only a few of the most important supporting details.

1. From the context clues, you can tell that *paraphrase* means about the same as ____________.

   topic   main idea   information   summarize

Read the paragraph and then complete the items that follow.

The Spanish people had many reasons for coming to North America. Beginning in the late 1400s, Spain's king and queen sent some men to explore and conquer the New World. These **conquistadors** came in search of gold and other riches to send back to Spain. Missionaries traveled with the explorers. The goal of the missionaries was to spread their religious beliefs and convert the people of North America to Catholicism. Religious communities called missions were established, and settlements grew up around them.

2. Highlight or underline the topic sentence, if there is one.

3. The Spanish people had many reasons for coming to North America. What were they? Mark each reason with a check mark.

_____ to search for riches to send to Spain

_____ beginning in the late 1400s

_____ to convert the people to Catholicism

_____ religious communities are called missions

_____ to colonize the New World

4. Fill in the circle next to the best title for the selection.

- ◯ Early Explorers of North and South America
- ◯ Why the Spanish Came to North America
- ◯ The King and Queen of Spain
- ◯ How Missions Become Settlements

5. From the context clues, you can tell that conquistadors are _________.

missionaries conquerors teachers slaves

6. Complete the analogy. January : beginning :: July : _________

ending fireworks middle summer

7. Arrange these words from general to specific. Number 1 is the most general; number 5 is the most specific.

____ Geography
____ Central Valley, CA
____ valleys in the West
__1__ school subjects
_____ landforms in North America

8. In a well-written passage, all the sentences support the

______________________ ________________________.

Lesson #4

Context Clues

Sometimes, passages contain new or difficult vocabulary. However, you can figure out the meaning of most words by using context clues. **Context clues** may be synonyms, antonyms, or definitions within the sentence or in nearby sentences. These clues explain the unknown word. (See the *Help Pages* in this book for more examples of context clues.)

Read the selection and pay attention to any unfamiliar words. Look for nearby clues that will help you to figure out the meaning of the new words.

Most experts agree about study tips for students, but what about playing music while studying? This is a **controversial** topic. Some people think it is fine to listen to **classical** background music, while others believe listening to music works against a student's powers of concentration. If a student chooses to play music while studying, soft classical music without **lyrics** is best. Music with no lyrics is less distracting than other types of music. The words of a song tend to mix with the words that a student is reading or trying to memorize. For many people, any kind of noise — even music they like — may weaken **cognitive function**. For others, a certain type of music may help their brains to work better.

1. A *controversial* topic is something that ________.
   A) people have different opinions about
   B) people agree about
   C) is recommended
   D) people need for studying

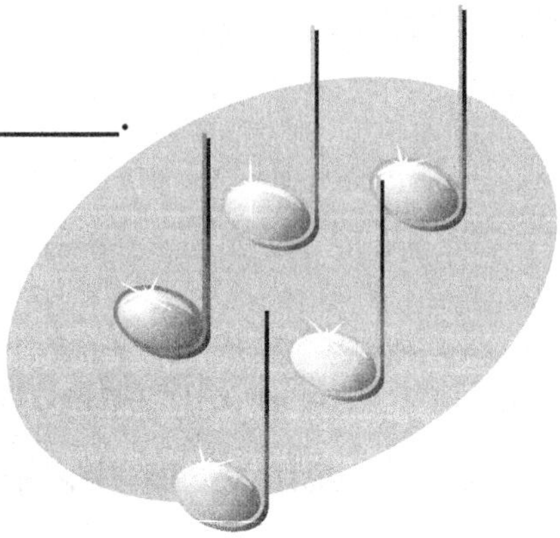

2. Musical *lyrics* are ________.

   notes instruments words thinking

3. From the context clues, you can tell that *cognitive function* probably has to do with ______.

   A) the work of the mind
   B) a subject in school
   C) music without words
   D) background noise

4. According to the paragraph, what is an advantage of classical music?

   A) Most people prefer classical music.
   B) Classical music costs less money.
   C) The words of classical music are in another language.
   D) Classical music is less distracting than other types of music.

5. What is the main idea of the paragraph?

   A) Everyone has different study habits.
   B) Classical music is better than pop or rock and roll music.
   C) It may or may not be a good idea to listen to music while studying.
   D) The brain works best with a little background music.

6. What should be included in a well-written summary?

   A) the main idea
   B) information written in your own words
   C) only a few supporting details
   D) all of the above

7. To find the main idea, ask, "______________________________

   ____?"

8. Choose the word that best completes the analogy.

   teeth : mouth :: keys : ________

   door   piano   notes   gums

Lesson #5

Cause and Effect

Every effect has a cause. An **effect** is a consequence, or something that happened, and the **cause** explains why it happened. Below are some clue words that can alert you to a cause-effect statement.

as a result	due to	thus	given that	that is why
because	since	hence	while	for that reason
consequently	so	and so	therefore	then

1 – 2. A cause-effect statement has two parts (the cause and the effect), and either part can come first. Here are some examples.

A) The volcano began to smolder, so local authorities evacuated the residents of the nearby town.

B) The sky was blackened since the volcano had been spewing hot ash and flame for days.

- Which example states the cause first? __________
- Which example states the effect first? __________

Some analogies are based on cause and effect. There is a cause-effect relationship between each set of words. Here is an example:

volcanic eruption : magma flow :: tremor : avalanche

A volcanic eruption causes a magma flow. A tremor causes an avalanche.

Read each sentence. Draw one line under the cause and two lines under the effect.

3. Because of the November election, a new mayor will preside over the city.

4. The new mayor is in favor of recycling; hence, a curbside recycling program will begin in January.

Read the sentences. Use context clues to determine the meaning of each underlined word.

5. The combination of screeching animals and guitar tuning created an unbearable dissonance that made Trevor cover his ears.

   jarring sound   fist fight

   soft sound   type of song

6. Our meeting that day was fortuitous. I had not planned to run into you, but it turned out to be the best thing that happened all day!

   wealthy   unfortunate

   accidental and lucky   planned

7. To ___________ means to restate the main idea and the most important details in your own words.

   summarize   paraphrase   both of these

8. Which type of reference book lists words in alphabetical order and gives synonyms for each word? (See the *Help Pages* if you are not sure.)

   thesaurus   almanac

   atlas   none of these

Lesson #6

The "Zipperless Zipper"

The invention of Velcro was the direct result of an encounter with Mother Nature. In 1948, a Swiss engineer, George de Mestral, returned from a hike in the Alps with his dog. Both man and dog were covered with burrs, the prickly parts of plant seeds. George de Mestral was a curious inventor. He decided to look at the burrs under his microscope, and he noticed that that burrs contained tiny hooks. The hooks clung to the loops of fabric in his pants and in the dog's fur. George de Mestral immediately thought of a two-sided fastener, consisting of a hook and loop.

Of course, de Mestral's idea was unconventional and was not immediately accepted. Eventually, however, the **entrepreneur** took his idea to a textile weaver in France. The weaver took the idea seriously, and the Velcro fastener was patented in 1955. Today, Velcro is a trademarked term that has become a **generic** household word. Velcro is used in countless products, and Velcro Industries is a multimillion dollar business, all because of a walk through the mountains.

1. Locate and underline the topic sentence in the first paragraph.

2. Which of these is the best summary of the second paragraph?

   ◯ The French are more open to new ideas than are the Swiss.

   ◯ Although de Mestral's idea was not accepted at first, Velcro is a multi-million dollar business today.

   ◯ You can do many cool things with Velcro.

   ◯ George de Mestral was a genius!

3. Why is the paragraph titled "The 'Zipperless Zipper' "?

   A) Velcro is a synonym for *zipper*.

   B) George de Mestral invented Velcro and the zipper.

   C) George de Mestral's dog was covered in burrs.

   D) Velcro works like a zipper because it fastens things together.

4. Context clues tell you that *entrepreneur* names someone who ______.

   A) starts out as an engineer
   B) turns an idea into a business
   C) is not very busy
   D) enjoys hiking with a dog

5. Which word means about the same as *generic*? Use context clues.

   common rare new invented

Write C for **cause** or E for **effect**.

6. ____ A French textile weaver took George de Mestral's idea seriously.

7. ____ As a result, the Velcro fastener was patented in 1955.

8. Put the words below into the graphic organizer. List them from most general (top) to most specific (bottom).

   George de Mestral Inventors Swiss Inventors

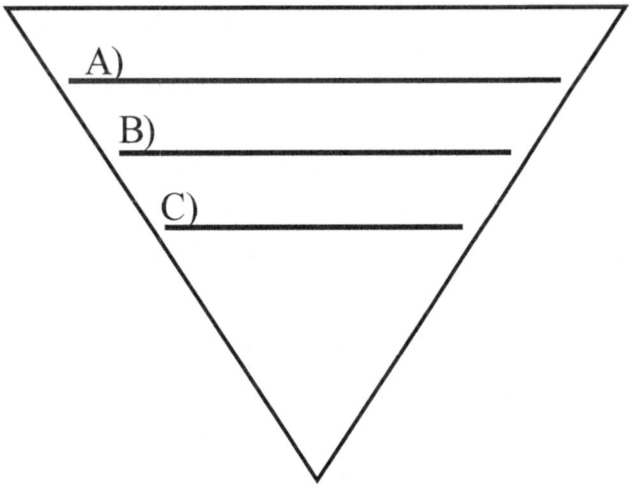

Study Strategy Remember, you can use an **inverted pyramid** to organize information from general to specific.

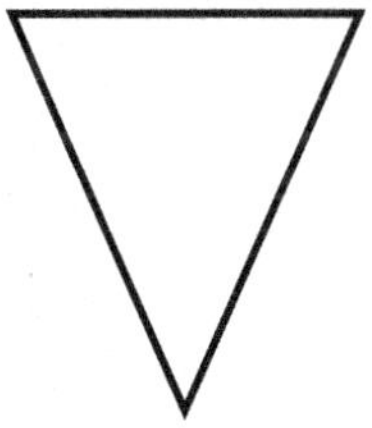

Lesson #7

Fact and Opinion

A fact is something that can be proven; an opinion cannot. Any statement may be purely factual, or it may simply be someone's personal viewpoint. Sometimes a statement contains a little of both. Here are some examples:

- **Fact**: The Rock and Roll Hall of Fame and Museum is located in Cleveland, Ohio.
- **Opinion**: The Rock and Roll Hall of Fame is an excellent place for education about the arts.
- **Both**: Aretha Franklin, <u>one of the greatest singers of all time</u>, was the first woman inducted into the Rock and Roll Hall of Fame.

In the last statement, the opinion part is underlined. Many people believe that Aretha Franklin is one of the greatest singers of all time, but this is a viewpoint. No one can prove it. The other part of the sentence can be proven by checking the documents at the Rock and Roll Hall of Fame and Museum.

Read each statement. Write F if it is a **fact** or O if it is an **opinion**.

1. ____ The state of Georgia was named in honor of King George II of England.
2. ____ Georgia is one of the best places to find delicious peaches.
3. ____ The state of West Virginia has an area of about 24,000 square miles.

Study Strategy When you are taking a test and you get stuck, take an educated guess. Then move on to the next question. An **educated guess** is a guess that is based on your previous knowledge and experience. Come back later and check your answer once you become "unstuck."

Each statement below has both fact and opinion. Draw a line under the part that states an opinion in each sentence.

4. West Virginia is an excellent place for hiking because the state has thirty-five state parks and seven state forests.

5. The Jefferson National Forest, located in Virginia, is most vibrant and beautiful during the peak of autumn.

6. In 2011, a 65-foot tall tree was brought to Washington, D.C., from Stanislaus National Forest in California; this magnificent tree was the most stunning Christmas tree ever!

Read the sentences. Use context clues to decide the meaning of the underlined words.

7. The events will happen in this <u>sequence</u>: first, the relay races; next, the sack races. Then, we will form two lines for the water balloon toss.

   Which of these means about the same as *sequence*?

   order day circle time

8. Your parents must be in their seats by 7:30 p.m. When you talk to your parents, please <u>convey</u> the importance of arriving on time for the play.

   Which of these means about the same as *convey*?

   appear

   invite

   make known

   audience

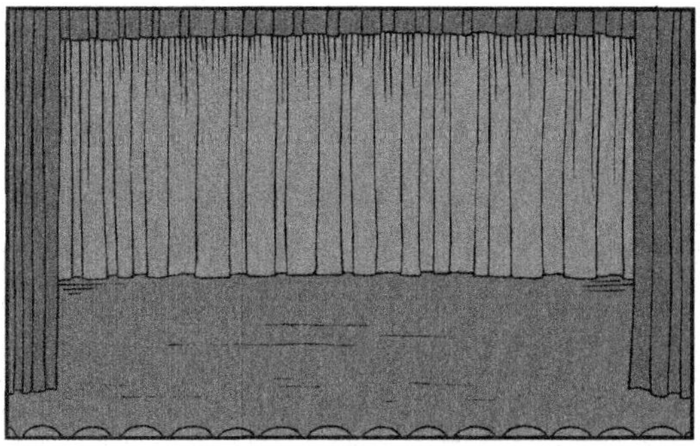

Lesson #8

Using Mnemonic Devices

A **mnemonic** (ni•**mon**•ik) is a memory strategy. It can help you to memorize the names of state capitals or remember items on a grocery list. A mnemonic can be a rhyme or song; it can even be a picture in your mind. Mnemonics do not have to make sense.

One common form of mnemonic is an acronym. An **acronym** is a word that is made from the first initials of the words you need to remember. It can be a nonsense word or an actual word. When the order does not matter, you can rearrange letters to form a real word. Below are the steps for creating an acronym.

- Make a list of the words you need to memorize.
- Underline the first letter of each word.
- Arrange the letters to form a real or a nonsense word.

Example: SCUBA = **S**elf-**C**ontained **U**nderwater **B**reathing **A**pparatus.

1. Underline or highlight the definitions for *mnemonic* and *acronym.*

Match each acronym with the information it will help you to remember.

HOMES NEWS PEN PALE

2. __________ the stages of metamorphosis (egg, larva, pupa, adult)

3. __________ the Great Lakes (Huron, Ontario, Michigan, Erie, Superior)

4. __________ the parts of an atom (proton, neutron, electron)

5. __________ the four directions (north, south, east, west)

An **acrostic** is an acronym sentence that helps you to memorize information. Take the first letter of each word in your study list and think of a word for each one. Then arrange the words to make a sentence.

Example: An **acrostic** for the seven continents would be this:
"Eat an apple as a nighttime snack." = Europe, Antarctica, Africa, Asia, Australia, North America, South America

6. Match each mnemonic with the information it will help you to remember.

A) Will a jolly man make a jolly visitor?

B) Any skunk is a pest.

C) My very educated mother just served us nachos.

_____ the planets in our solar system (Mercury, Venus, Earth, Mars, Jupiter, Saturn, Uranus, Neptune)

_____ the oceans of the world (Antarctic, Southern, Indian, Atlantic, Pacific)

_____ the first eight presidents (Washington, Adams, Jefferson, Madison, Monroe, Adams, Jackson, Van Buren)

Read each statement. Write F if it is a **fact** or O if it is an **opinion**.

7. _____ Seven United States presidents were born in Ohio.

8. _____ The greatest United States presidents were elected during the Twentieth Century.

Study Strategy
Be very careful when marking a T or an F as your answer. Be sure the teacher can tell what the letter is. If your letter is not clear, the item may be marked wrong.

Lesson #9

Other Memory Strategies

Besides acronyms and acronym sentences, there are many other strategies for remembering facts. **Rhyming** can make memorizing fun. You can make up songs, wordplay, and poems to help you memorize everything from math facts to spelling rules.

Grouping is a way to learn a list of facts. For example, if you need to memorize the names of the fifty states, you can group them according to their regions. Then, you only need to learn about a dozen at a time.

Using **flashcards** is another tried and true method of memorizing — especially for things like math facts and new vocabulary. Make your own set of flashcards by writing a fact or question on one side and the answer on the other side. You can also add a drawing or symbol that may help to trigger your memory.

Using a drawing or symbol is another memory strategy. **Visualization** is the name for a mental image or picture you see in your mind that can help you learn what you need to know. You can find more information about memory strategies in the *Help Pages.*

Which memory device is used in these sentences?

1. 1959 was the date when Hawaii became a state.

   rhyming acronym grouping all of these

2. Using a drawing or symbol as a way to remember is called ____.

   rhyming acronym grouping visualization

3. Which of these is the best strategy for memorizing math facts?

   flashcards acronyms acrostics analogies

Study Strategy You can also use visualization techniques to relax right before a test. Close your eyes. Take a few very deep breaths. Picture yourself in a place that is very calming. Visualize yourself relaxing there. It really works!

4. Which mnemonic would be best for memorizing the thirteen colonies?

Virginia, Massachusetts, New Hampshire, Maryland, Connecticut, Rhode Island, Delaware, North Carolina, South Carolina, New Jersey, New York, Pennsylvania, Georgia

- ◯ Virginia makes new models complete with paper and glue. She never makes a mistake.
- ◯ Vegetables make nifty snacks and coconuts ripen under the southern sun.
- ◯ Very many cute monkeys ride goats & donkeys; penguins never shout, "New, new, new!"

5. Which of these is another good strategy for memorizing the names of the thirteen colonies?

using flashcards   grouping   visualization   all of these

6. Which is the best mnemonic for memorizing the layers of Earth? (crust, mantle, outer core, inner core)

- ◯ COMICC
- ◯ Many orange crates can be carried in cars.
- ◯ Crates of money outweigh common inner tubes.
- ◯ Chrissy, my other cat, is comical.

7. Read the statement:

Crustaceans are more interesting than reptiles because crustaceans have hard shells, antennae, and eyes at the end of stalks.

Does it contain a fact, an opinion, or both? ________________

8. Choose the word that best completes the analogy. Use a dictionary if you need help.

elevate : raise :: sink : ________

kitchen   increase   descend   float

Lesson #10

Read the paragraph and answer the questions below.

The Japanese people have beautiful traditions for remembering their loved ones who have died. Many Japanese families keep altars in their homes as a way to honor their **ancestors**. An altar is a special place. It may be a table, a small room, or a corner of a room. An altar may be **adorned** with incense, fresh food, and flowers, as well as photographs of relatives who have died. Each year, Japanese people observe a holiday called the Bon Festival or Oban, a time of celebration in honor of the ancestors. It is also called the Feast of the Lanterns. People may float candles down a river or light lanterns in their homes. The lighted candles or lanterns represent the spirits of the ancestors. During the festival, people remember their loved ones and thank them for all they did to make life better for future generations.

1. Underline the topic sentence if there is one.

2. Why is the Bon Festival also called the Feast of the Lanterns?

   A) People may light lanterns in their homes.

   B) Lanterns represent the spirits of the ancestors.

   C) both A and B

   D) information not given

3. A) Another word for family members who lived before us is ________.

   altars traditions ancestors Japanese

   B) From the context clues, you can tell that *adorned* means ________.

   torn down built worshipped decorated

4. Three of these words are synonyms. Cross out the one that does not belong.

holiday festival celebration tradition

5. Which <u>saying</u> goes best with the main idea of the paragraph?

- ◯ When you are thirsty, it is too late to think about digging a well.
- ◯ We never miss the water until the well runs dry.
- ◯ When you are drinking water from a well, think about the person who dug the well long ago.
- ◯ When the well is deep, the water must be lifted higher.

6. Which mnemonic device is represented? ____________________

Red sky at morning, sailors' warning;

red sky at night, sailors' delight.

7. In a well-written passage, all the sentences support the ____________________.

8. In 2011, a high magnitude earthquake occurred near the coast of Japan. The earthquake triggered a 23-foot high wave, called a tsunami, which hit the coastline afterwards.

The earthquake was (a cause / an effect), and the tsunami was (a cause / an effect).

Lesson #11

Graphic Organizers: Tables and Charts

Tables and **charts** are meant to organize large amounts of data and make data easier to read. When you are reading a table or chart, glance over the whole thing first. Find the title; it will give the main idea. Then, read the heading for each column. The headings tell what information is in each column. Finally, read the information both **horizontally** (across) and **vertically** (up and down).

Study the chart. Use the information to complete the first four items.

Yosemite National Park Goes Solar	
Size of solar panels	8 ft. x 12 ft.
Number of panels	2,800
Amount of power provided	800,000 kWh*
Cost of project	$5.8 million
Estimated savings	$50,000 per year
Project completion	June 2011
(* kWh = kilowatt-hours — the unit of measure for electricity used over time.)	

Source: www.mercedsunstar.com/2011/07/28/1985051/yosemite-park-offices-get-solar.html

1. According to the title, what is the new source of power in Yosemite Park?

   natural gas   solar power   a wind turbine   running water

2. Each solar panel is approximately the size of a _______.

   yardstick

   meter stick

   small bedroom

   city

3. When was the project due to be completed?

   ____

4. About how much power can the new source provide?

A) 50,000 dollars per year
B) 800,000 kilowatt hours per year
C) 2,800 panels
D) 48 square feet

5. Fill in the blanks to complete this rhyming mnemonic for remembering the number of days in each month. (Hint: December has thirty-one days.)

Thirty days have September,

April, June, and ______________________.

All the rest have thirty-one, except February

with twenty-eight days clear

and twenty-nine each leap ______________.

Read each statement. Write F if it is a **fact**, O if it is an **opinion**, or B if it is **both**.

6. _____ All of the National Parks should be working to reduce the amount of electricity produced by non-renewable resources.

7. _____ National Parks have offices, maintenance and storage facilities, and parking lots; these things are necessary for keeping the parks safe and clean.

8. _____ The power source project in Yosemite National Park was paid for with funding from the American Recovery and Reinvestment Act.

Lesson #12

Graphic Organizers: Three-Column Charts and Venn Diagrams

A three-column chart or Venn diagram compares two items that have some traits or characteristics in common, as well as some differences. Study the chart and use the information to complete the items below.

American Alligator	Both	American Crocodile
• species is thriving • lives in rivers, lakes, swamps, and marshes of the Southeast • excellent swimmer • averages 10 – 15 feet long • lives 35 – 50 years • feeds on fish, mammals, other reptiles (turtles, snakes) • may attack humans	• reptile • hatches from an egg • carnivore • predator	• species is endangered • lives in fresh or brackish waters of Central America and the Caribbean • averages 13 – 20 feet long • lives up to 70 years in the wild • feeds on fish, birds, crabs, insects, snails, frogs • unlikely to attack humans

1. Which of these would be the best title for the chart?

   Predators of North America   Reptiles that Kill
   Comparing Alligators and Crocodiles   Endangered Species

2. Which species is endangered?

   Alligators   Crocodiles   both   information not given

3. Which reptile prefers to live in fresh water only?

   Alligators   Crocodiles   both   information not given

A Venn diagram consists of two overlapping circles that show what the two items have in common as well as how they differ. There are lists of states in the diagram shown below, and the characteristics are "borders Canada" and "borders the Great Lakes." The states listed in the overlapping part border <u>both</u> Canada and the Great Lakes.

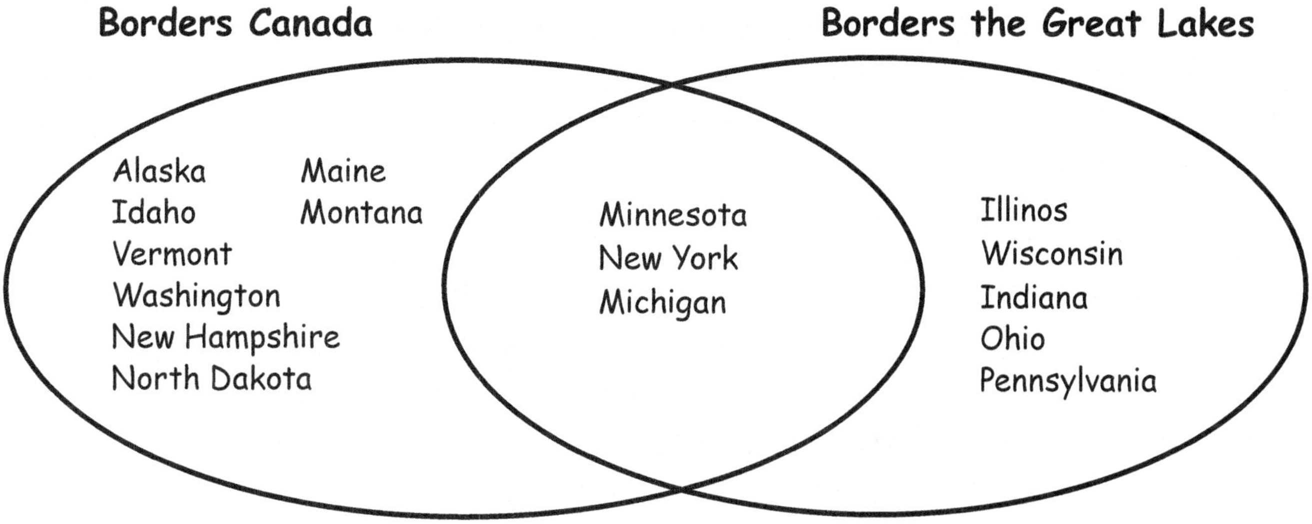

4. How many states border Canada? Remember to add the ones in the middle of the Venn diagram. __________

5. How many states border the Great Lakes? __________

6. How many states border both Canada and the Great Lakes? __________

Write C if the underlined part names a **cause** or E if it names an **effect**.

7. ____ Due to habitat loss, illegal hunting, and pet trade, <u>many tortoises and freshwater turtles are endangered</u>.

8. ____ Scientists are learning more about the migration of leatherback turtles because <u>they have new technologies like satellite tracking devices</u>.

Lesson #13

Graphic Organizers: Timelines

A **timeline** shows dates and events in an organized manner. It is arranged in **chronological order**, the order in which the events happened. A timeline can be displayed **vertically** (up and down) or **horizontally** (left to right). Usually, a timeline includes a title that tells about the information in the timeline. Below is a vertical timeline. Study the details and use it to complete the items that follow.

1867	U.S. purchases Alaska from Russia
1872	Gold is discovered in Sitka
1876	Gold is discovered in Juneau
1884	Alaska becomes a U.S. territory
1897–1900	Klondike Gold Rush (more than 100,000 prospectors)
1900	Juneau becomes the new capital of Alaska White Pass and Yukon Railroad are completed
1925	Dog sled teams led by Balto and Togo travel for 5 days to deliver medicine to diphtheria epidemic areas
1959	Alaska becomes the 49th U.S. state

1. Which of these would be the best title for the timeline?

The Gold Rush in North America | Railroads in the Yukon

High Points in Alaska's History | Alaska and Hawaii

Study Strategy A timeline is a good tool to use when writing a report. If you are given many dates, names, and events, you can first arrange them on a visual organizer. Then begin to write chronologically about the various events.

2. Number these items from 1 – 5 in the order in which they occurred. Number one occurred first.

    _____ Balto's and Togo's teams delivered medicine
    _____ Alaska became a state
    _____ the Klondike Gold Rush
    _____ gold was discovered in Sitka
    _____ Juneau became the capital of Alaska

3. What country was Alaska part of before it became the 49th state?

    Canada   Russia   Iceland   Mexico

4. What valuable resource led over 100,000 people to Alaska at the turn of the century? _______________

5. A timeline is arranged in __________ order.

    alphabetical   vertical   horizontal   chronological

6. Which of these is the best mnemonic for remembering the vertebrate groups? (amphibians, birds, fish, reptiles, mammals)

    BARNS   FRAMB   RAFAR   BRAME

7. Which of these is the best type of graphic organizer for showing similarities and differences between two things?

    timeline   bar graph   Venn diagram   acronym

8. Write F for **fact**, O for **opinion**, or B for **both**. Remember, a fact can be proven.

    _____ Alaska is the only U.S. state that has part of its land in the Eastern Hemisphere.

    _____ During certain times of the year, the sun does not set in some parts of Alaska.

Lesson #14

Graphic Organizers: Graphs

There are many different types of graphs — pie graphs, line graphs, bar graphs, and pictographs, just to name a few. Each type of graph presents information a little differently, but all graphs are meant to display a large amount of information at a glance. Read a graph's title, captions, and labels; these will tell you about the data on the graph.

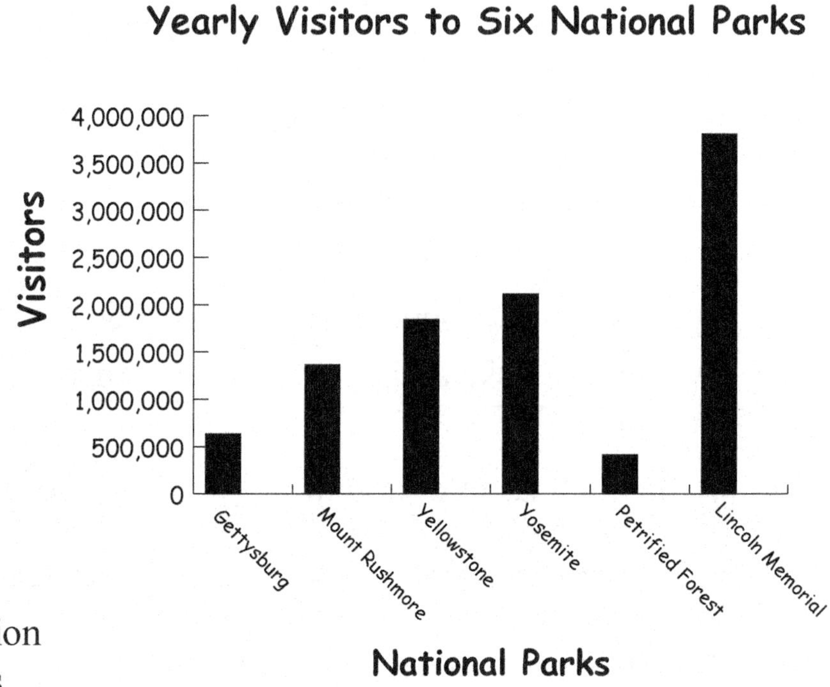

A bar graph compares the data from several items. Study this bar graph and use the information to complete the following items.

1. The information in the graph shows the number of _______.
   A) national parks there are in the United States
   B) people who have visited certain parks in a single year
   C) visitors to all of the parks in the United States
   D) people who have visited certain parks since they first opened

2. Which parks had more than a million visitors in a single year?

   Lincoln Memorial   Mount Rushmore   Petrified Forest
   Yellowstone   Yosemite   none of these

3. Which park had the fewest visitors? ______________________

4. Which conclusion can you draw from information in the graph on the previous page?

   A) There are more national parks in the West.
   B) People are not interested in the Petrified Forest.
   C) It is very expensive to visit Gettysburg National Park.
   D) The Lincoln Memorial is the most popular of the six parks on the graph.

A **line graph** is best for showing trends or change over time. Study this line graph and use the information in it to complete the following items.

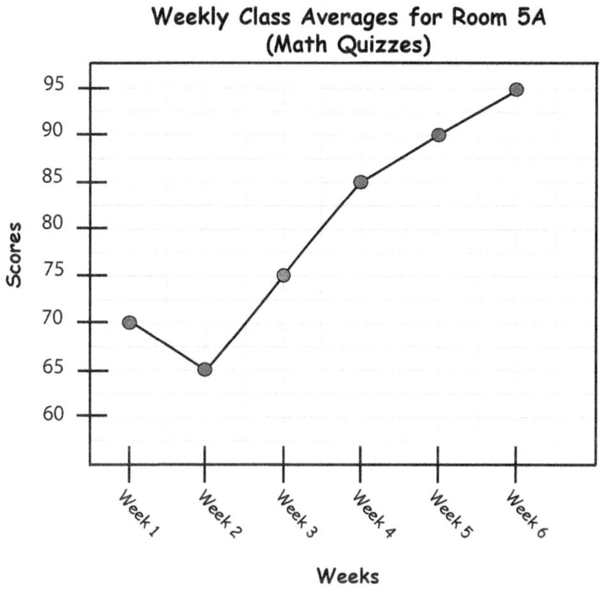

5. What does this graph show?

   A) the average scores of six different students
   B) the average quiz scores of a single class over six weeks
   C) the average number of items on a test over time

6. A line graph is best for ________.

   A) showing how scores increase or decrease over time
   B) listing the number of days in a school year
   C) comparing and contrasting two objects

7. The average quiz scores for Room 5A mostly ____________ over time.

   A) stayed the same
   B) increased
   C) decreased
   D) information not given

8. The purpose of a graph is to ________.

   A) show events in the order in which they happened
   B) display a large amount of information at a glance
   C) give synonyms and antonyms of a word
   D) display a title and a caption

Lesson #15

A **pie graph** shows parts of a whole. Study the graph and use the information in it to complete the following items.

A **primary language** is a person's first or main language. Many people speak more than one language, but the pie graph only counts primary languages. The "other" category covers any other language not shown in one of the segments of the graph.

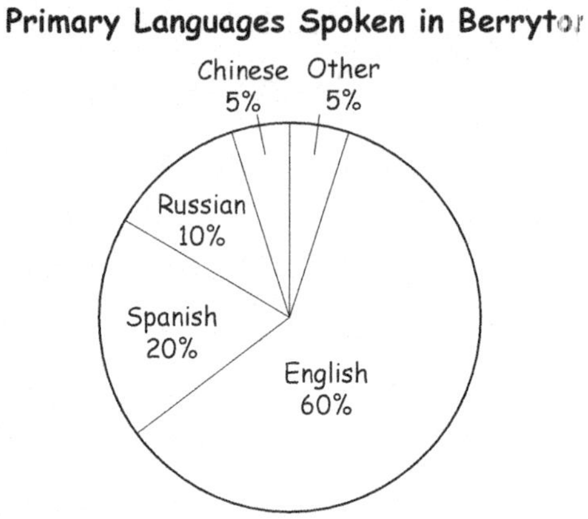

1. Which of these is definitely true?

_____ No one in Berryton speaks Japanese.
_____ Most people in Berryton speak more than one Language.
_____ At least half the people in Berryton speak English.

2. All of the parts or segments of a pie graph add up to ______.

100%   the majority   at least half   a different amount

3. A pie graph is best for ________.

A) showing changes over time
B) listing events in chronological order
C) showing parts of a whole
D) all of these

Study Strategy You can find many graphs, charts, and diagrams used in everyday life. For one week, keep track of all the graphic organizers you see in newspapers, magazines, and on television. You may be surprised at how many there are!

A **pictograph** is like a bar graph but with symbols that stand for a certain things. Usually a key or legend shows the value of each symbol. Study this pictograph and use the information in it to complete the following items.

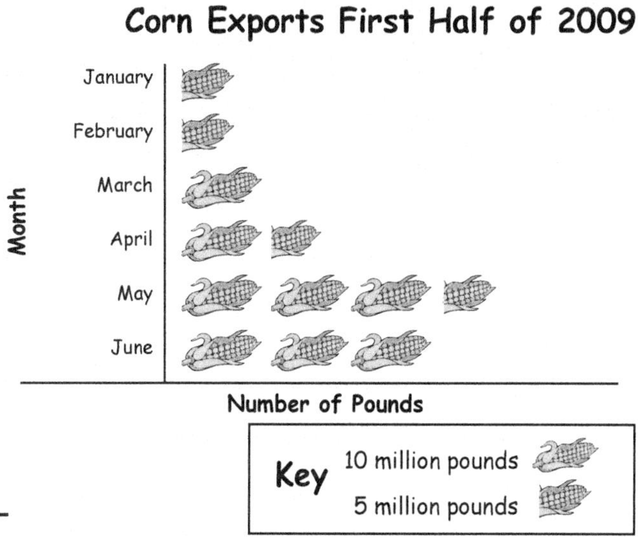

4. What does each ear of corn on the pictograph represent?

   A) a bushel of corn
   B) a million pounds of corn
   C) a ton of corn
   D) ten million pounds of corn

5. How much corn was exported during April? ________

6. What information is missing from the pictograph?

   the title　　a key or legend　　name of the country exporting corn

7. Which conclusion can you draw by studying the graph?

   A) There are 70 pounds of corn in a bushel.
   B) Most of the corn is grown in May.
   C) No corn is exported during July or August.
   D) The amount of corn exported in May is equal to the total for January, February, March, and April.

8. Draw a line to match each type of graph with its clue.

line graph	shows parts of a whole
bar or pictograph	shows trends or change over time
pie or circle graph	compares the data from several items

Lesson #16

Diagrams

Diagrams are an important part of many textbooks, especially science texts. A **diagram** is a drawing with parts that are labeled. A diagram may show a whole object or just a part of something. For example, the diagrams shown below are partial drawings of two different types of elephants.

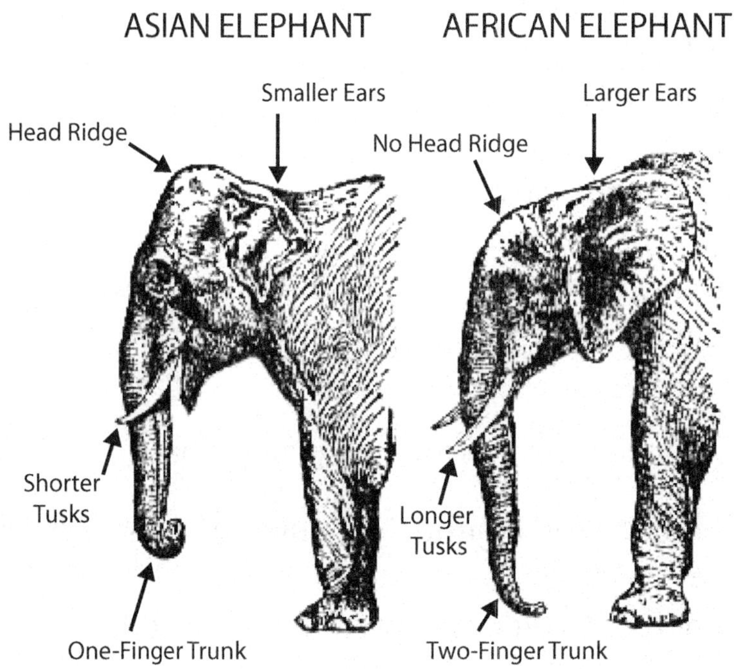

1. Both types of elephants have ___________.

   head ridges   two-fingered trunks   tusks   all of these

2. One physical difference between an African elephant and an Asian elephant is the size of their ___________.

   habitats   ears   eyes   appetites

3. According to the diagram at the right, an insect has

   _____ body segments and ______ pairs of legs.

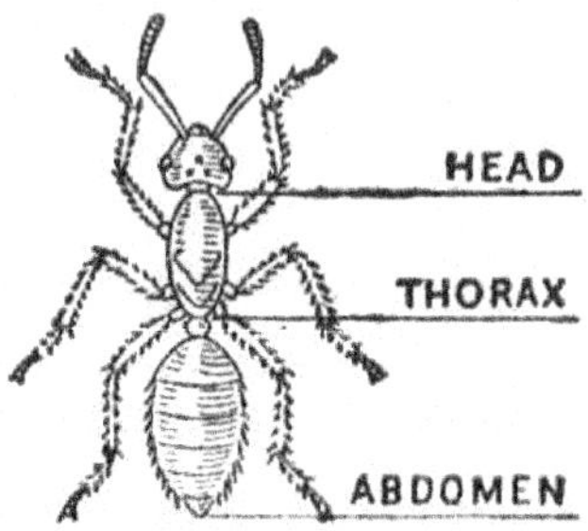

Insect

4. Which of these is an example of a rhyming mnemonic?

   A) India is big, but Africa is bigger, and that's true of their elephants, easy to figure!
   B) **I** before **e**, except after **c** or when sounded like **ā**, as in **neighbor** and **weigh**
   C) lefty loosey, righty tighty
   D) all of these

The **demographics** of an area give information about the people who live there. Study the chart of demographics for Dayton, Washington, and use the information to complete the following items.

5. You can tell from the information in the chart that _____ is an important part of the economy in Dayton, Washington.

   fishing

   car manufacturing

   farming

   recycling

Demographics of Dayton, Washington

Population	2,400
Historic Properties	more than 120
County Area	553,600 acres
Farmed Acres	201,000 acres
Forest Acres	200,000 acres
Rangeland and Other	152,000 acres
Major Crop	Wheat
Growing Season	160 days
Annual Rainfall	11 - 26 inches
Average Temperatures	summer: 72°F, winter: 28°F

Source: http://www.daytonwa.com/html/about_dayton.html

6. How much land is set aside for forests in Dayton, Washington? ______________________

7. What is the major agricultural (farming) product of Dayton? ______________________

8. How long is the growing season? ______________________

Lesson #17

Comparing African and Asian Elephants

African and Asian elephants are the largest land animals on Earth, and there are many similarities between the two. Both are mammals; they are herbivores (plant eaters), and they live in herds. Females of both species are called cows, and the males are called bulls. Elephants like to be near water where they can cool off, get a drink, and play. They enjoy squirting water from their trunks. Both types of elephants have trunks, which are really their noses. Both animals use their trunks for breathing and smelling; they are also used for grabbing, drinking, and making a sound like a trumpet.

African elephants are larger and have bigger ears than Asian elephants. Some people think the African elephant's ears have the shape of Africa. Both the cows and bulls have tusks, and they have round smooth heads. At the tip of an African elephant's trunk are two finger-like extensions that allow them to grasp things. African elephants may live for 70 years, and they are a threatened species.

Asian elephants are a little smaller, and they have smaller, more rounded ears. Their heads have two humps, and only the males have visible tusks. Asian elephants also have trunks, but their trunks have just one finger-like extension at the end. The Asian elephant may live for a period of up to 60 years and is a highly endangered species.

1. Reread the first paragraph. Highlight or underline seven common characteristics of African and Asian elephants.

2. Reread the second paragraph. Highlight or underline seven characteristics that are unique to the African elephant.

3. Reread the third paragraph. Highlight or underline seven characteristics that are unique to the Asian elephant.

4 – 8. Summarize the paragraphs by completing the three-column chart. Fill in seven details in each of the three sections.

African Elephant	Both	Asian Elephant

Study Strategy One way to keep organized is to have a special assignment notebook for your homework and project schedules only. Use it daily to write down assignments. Check your notebook several times a day to be sure you've recorded and completed all your work.

Lesson #18

Test-Taking Strategies and Tips

To prepare for a test, use all of the strategies you have learned so far: finding the main idea, using context clues, making use of mnemonics and other memory devices, and managing information with graphic organizers. These things help you to study and prepare for a test ahead of time.

On the day of the test, when you receive the test, the two most important strategies for doing well are...

1) **Listen to or read directions carefully,** and

2) **Read each item completely before writing an answer.**

It is also very important to write legibly, manage your time, and reread all of your answers to make sure you have done your best before handing in your test. You will find a list of study and test-taking strategies and tips in the *Help Pages* at the back of this book.

1 – 4. Draw a line to match each phrase on the left with its ending on the right.

If any part of a true or false statement is false,	even if you have to make a guess.
After you have looked over a test,	the entire statement is false.
Before the test begins, make sure	begin by doing the easiest items first.
Complete every item on the test	you know how many minutes you have, so you can manage your time.

5. On any type of test, it is important to _________, so that you can get full credit for your work.

A) write neatly
B) follow the directions
C) read everything
D) do all of these things

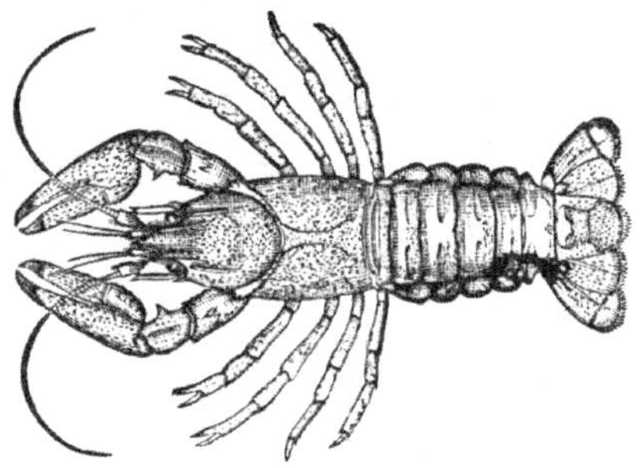

The crayfish has bilateral symmetry, which means that it has two matching sides.

The diagram below shows just one side of a crayfish.

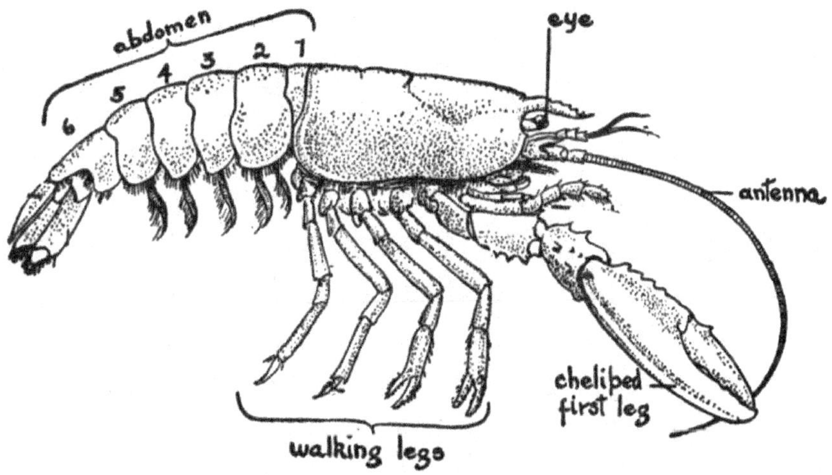

6. How many sections make up the abdomen of the crayfish? ____________________

7. Altogether, how many walking legs are there on the body of the crayfish? ____________________

8. How many antennae does the crayfish have? ____________________

Lesson #19

Essay Writing

The most important part of completing an essay item is to carefully read the prompt so you know exactly what you are asked to do. Read the prompt several times and pay attention to key words such as "explain," "prove," "summarize," "describe," "illustrate," and "review." Key words are important because each word asks you to do something different. A good strategy is to underline the key words immediately; then think about exactly what the words are asking you to do.

Follow these steps when responding to an essay item:

- Read the prompt several times. Underline key words.
- Rephrase the prompt to form a topic sentence for your essay.
- Brainstorm a list of topics to discuss in your essay.
- Organize your thoughts in a brief outline.
- Write the essay. Begin with a topic sentence and follow your outline.
- Review your essay for clarity, sense, spelling, and grammar.

Read the essay prompt below. Then complete the next two items.

> Name three problems the early colonists faced; then describe how they overcame each one.

1. What are two things that the prompt asks you to do?

_____ describe three solutions _____ name three problems

_____ list the names of the colonies _____ write a summary

2. Always <u>rephrase</u> the prompt to form a topic sentence for your essay. Which of these would be the best topic sentence for the essay item?

   A) Native Americans taught some of the early colonists how to plant crops and hunt for food.
   B) The early colonists had many difficulties settling in once they left England.
   C) Three of the problems that the early colonists faced were disease, hunger, and isolation.
   D) The voyage was very difficult and the Puritans arrived in America weak and hungry.

3. Read the directions below. Select the **key words.**

   Summarize the events that happened in Chapter One.

   Then explain what you think will happen next.

Each statement below contains both fact and opinion. Draw a line under the part of each sentence that states an opinion.

4. Henry Ford became the greatest genius of the twentieth century when he implemented the assembly line for car manufacturing.

5. Henry Ford grew up on a farm, but his ideas and innovations affected city life beyond what anyone could have imagined.

6. Everyone should know that Henry Ford's company manufactured the Model T.

Write C if the underlined part names a **cause** or E if it names an **effect.**

7. _____ In an industrialized America, machines can outperform human actions; as a result, <u>there are fewer jobs</u>.

8. _____ <u>Today, manufacturing is more efficient and profitable</u> due to the development of assembly lines and interchangeable parts.

Lesson #20

Read the paragraphs before completing the items that follow.

Kittens love to play. They like to **stalk**, bite, and bat their paws. This kind of play can be **exasperating** to the kitten's owner, but kittens are not just playing for fun. They act this way by **instinct**. By playing, kittens learn to hunt. Even though house cats are mostly **tame**, they still have some of the instincts of wild cats, and one of those instincts is hunting. When cats and kittens play, they are practicing for the real thing.

Many cat owners know that this hunting practice pays off. It is not uncommon for someone with an outdoor cat to find a "gift" left on the porch. The "gift" can be a dead bird, mouse, or chipmunk. So, if you get a newborn kitten, do it a favor and get it a toy that looks like a mouse. That will make their play more exciting!

1. Which of these best explains the main idea of the selection?

   A) A pet owner should know that kittens need a lot of attention.
   B) When kittens are playing, they are acting out the instinct to hunt.
   C) A newborn kitten needs to have toys that look like small animals.
   D) The owner of a kitten should be careful because kittens bite!

Find the bolded words and use context clues to answer these questions.

2. Which word names a behavior that an animal has without being taught? ______________________

3. Which word names the way a cat walks when it is hunting? ______________________

4. Which word describes a pet or an animal that is not wild? ______________________

5. Which of these means about the same as the word *exasperating*?

annoying   breathing   communicating   adorable

Parts of a Textbook

There are several important and helpful parts to a textbook: the **table of contents**, glossary, index, photos, maps, diagrams, and captions. The table of contents is in the front of the book. It is like an outline that lists each chapter or unit and the page number on which it begins. The **glossary** and **index** are in the back of the book and have words listed alphabetically. The glossary gives the meaning of each word, and the index tells where in the book you can find it. **Captions** are the words printed under photos and other graphics; they provide useful information. It is a good idea to take the time to study photos and graphics and to read the captions that go with them.

6 – 8. Choose the textbook part that goes with each hint.

- This lists all the units and their chapters in the book, along with page numbers.

  table of contents   glossary   index   captions

- This gives the meaning and definitions of vocabulary found in the book.

  table of contents   glossary   index   captions

- This is a description printed under photos or other graphics; it provides useful information.

  table of contents   glossary   index   captions

Lesson #21

Using Resources

You can find just about any information you are looking for on the Internet. In addition to the Internet, several other resources can help you in very specific ways. Choosing the proper resources will help you to do your best at writing a report or research paper. An **encyclopedia** will provide you with excellent information that has been written by experts. A **thesaurus** will help you to choose exactly the right words for what you want to say, and a **dictionary** will help you to say and use those words correctly. An **atlas** is a book of maps, and an **almanac** is an up-to-date book filled with facts and lists of names, dates, and places.

1 – 3. Write the name of each resource in the space next to its clue. You'll find the list of resources in the *Help Pages.*

Resource	Clue
	an electronic network that connects computers all over the world; a place to find electronic versions of all the other resources
	published yearly; a book of current facts, figures, dates, tables, and lists
	a book of synonyms and antonyms; used for finding the perfect word for exactly what you want to say
	a book of maps; shows continents, landforms, cities, states, countries, oceans, and other bodies of water
	words are listed in alphabetical order; listing provides the correct spelling, punctuation, origin, and meaning of the word
	volumes containing factual articles written by experts; topics are arranged in alphabetical order

Study Strategy

A good dictionary or a thesaurus can make an excellent birthday or holiday gift. Both are great investments because they are used often, and they last a very long time.

4. In a well-written passage, all sentences support the

______________________________________.

5. Which is the best type of graph for showing parts of a whole?

pictograph line graph pie graph double bar graph

6. Choose the word pair that best completes the analogy.

desert : dry :: ____________________

glacier : frozen cactus : prairie range : mountain ride : bike

7 – 8. A bar graph compares data. Use information in the table to create a bar graph comparing the weights of each type of produce.

Produce	pounds per bushel
Snap bean	30
Cucumber	48
Eggplant	33
Okra	26
Onion	57
Tomato	53

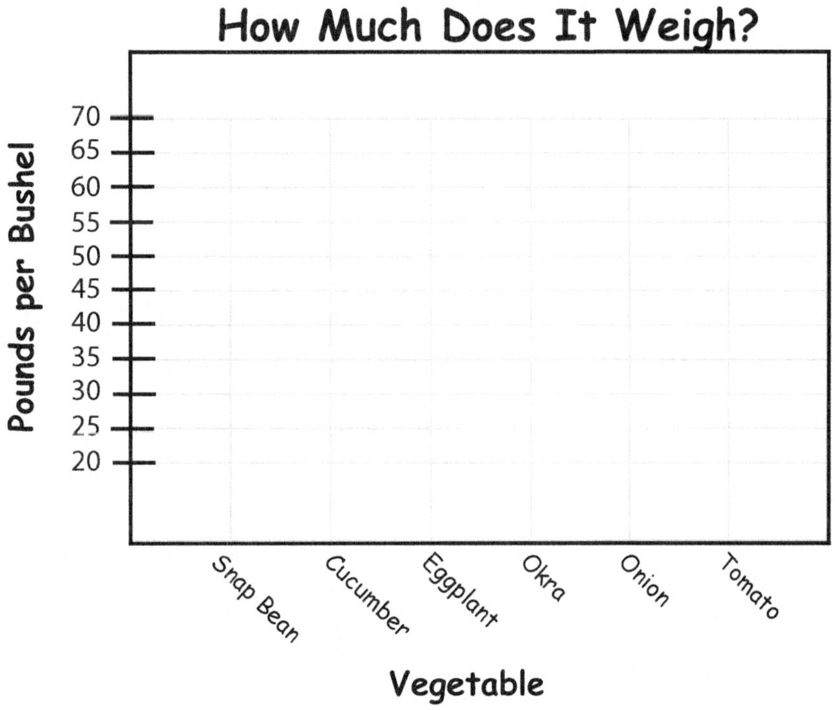

Lesson #22

Avoiding Plagiarism

Plagiarism is the illegal use of another person's words or ideas. Here are some examples:

- copying sentences directly from books, magazines, songs, or the Internet, and putting them in a paper with your name on it
- putting your name on a paper written by someone else
- using another person's words or ideas and calling them your own

There are specific ways to avoid plagiarism. The best way to avoid plagiarism is to put everything in your own words. Gather information from several sources, and then paraphrase what you have learned. Use your own words to write a summary of what you have read or heard.

Giving credit to the original writer or speaker is another way to avoid plagiarism. When you use someone else's ideas, always include that person's name, along with the book or article title. Restating exactly what someone else wrote or said is called quoting. In a quote, you write other people's words or ideas within quotation marks, but you always give them credit.

1. Draw a line under the definition of *plagiarism.*

2. Plagiarism is both _______.

   A) common and lawful

   B) easy and useful

   C) illegal and avoidable

   D) useless and allowable

3. When taking a test, circle the _______ in the directions and the questions if you are allowed to write on the test.

   mnemonic devices   resources   analogies   key words

4. Choose the word pair that best completes the analogy.

   knowledgeable : ignorant :: _______________

   crooked : straight   barbeque : summertime
   well-informed : lazy   swimming pool : heat wave

5. A) Which two parts of a textbook list words in alphabetical order?

   table of contents   index   glossary   list of graphics

   B) Which part gives the definitions of new words?

   table of contents   index   glossary   list of graphics

Complete the following statements about how to avoid plagiarism:

6. Gather ____________________ from ____________________ sources.

7. Then, ______________________________ what you have learned.

8. Use ______________________________ to write a summary of what you have learned.

Study Strategy Schools have rules against plagiarism. It is a serious offense to copy someone else's work and say it is your own. And, there are serious consequences. Understand the meaning of plagiarism and how to avoid it.

Lesson #23

Creating a Bibliography

One very important way to avoid plagiarism is to include a bibliography with your assignment. A **bibliography** is a listing of sources you used to gather information for your report, speech, or other project. A **source** can be a book, encyclopedia, newspaper, magazine, website, or interview.

A bibliography lists items in alphabetical order using the last names of the authors of all of the sources you used. If you used a book, give the author's name (last name first) and the title. The **author** is the writer of the material. If you used words or ideas from a website, give the author's name, the web address (also called the URL), and the date. If you interviewed someone, list that person's name and the date of the interview.

There are many ways to write a bibliography. Usually your teacher will give you directions for listing your sources. You can also find a template, or guide for writing a bibliography in the *Help Pages* at the back of this book. Here is the format for a book entry:

Author's Last name, First name. Title of Book. City: Publisher, Date.

Example:

Williams, Diana. Studying Global Warming. Juneau: Iceberg Press, 2011.

1. In what city was the book published? ______________________

2. What year was the book published? ______________________

3. A) What is the author's first name? ______________________

   B) What is the author's last name? ______________________

4. Check all that apply.

The purpose of a bibliography is to ________.

______ make your report longer

______ give credit to others

______ list your sources of information

______ avoid plagiarism

5. What is plagiarism? Check all that apply.

_____ copying and using another person's words without that person's permission

_____ putting your name on something you did not write

_____ using the Internet to do research

6. What are some ways to avoid plagiarism? Check all that apply.

_____ summarize and paraphrase, using your own words

_____ cite your sources in a bibliography

_____ use quotation marks around someone else's actual words

7. To figure out the main idea of a paragraph ask yourself, "_____________

____?"

8. Which resource is best for finding exactly the right words for what you want to say?

atlas

almanac

thesaurus

bibliography

Lesson #24

Read the paragraph below before completing the items that follow.

Animals may be dangerous because of their **massive** size, powerful jaws, sharp teeth, and large claws. On the other hand, size isn't everything. Very small animals are sometimes more dangerous than the most **ferocious** of **predators**. These are the animals that use venom to wound or kill their **prey**. Venom refers to poisons produced by wildlife, specifically poisons used for hunting or self defense. An animal does not have to be large or muscular when it has powerful venom to do all the work.

Some animals produce venom so **toxic** that they can injure or even kill others that are several times their size, including humans. Cobras, spiders, jellyfish, scorpions, and many other animals can be highly **venomous**. For example, the adorable platypus is an animal to look out for. This strange-looking, duck-billed creature is one of the world's only venomous mammals!

1. Which of these best tells the main idea of the selection?

   A) Wild animals can be extremely dangerous.
   B) The most dangerous animals are the biggest and have the sharpest teeth.
   C) The duck-billed platypus is the only mammal that uses venom.
   D) Even small animals can hunt and overpower their prey by using venom.

On its hind feet, the male platypus has sharp stingers that deliver strong venom.

2. Reread the bolded parts of the paragraph; then complete the items below.

A) What is meant by the phrase "several times their size"?

many times bigger   attacked over a period of time

born many times   as big as a human

B) Underline **three** words that are synonyms.

toxic   ferocious   venomous   poison   massive

3. From the context clues, you can tell that *predator* is about the same as a ________.

poison   victim   hunter   instinct

4. A word that means *very big* is_______.

massive   venomous   predator   ferocious

5. Which word means about the same as *ferocious*?

venomous   massive   violent   endangered

6. Another term for *prey* is __________.

strange-looking   victim   toxic   kill

7. Which pair best completes the analogy?   arid : dry :: ___________

humid : sunny   chilly : cold   muggy : desert-like   balmy : wintry

8. Write F if the statement is a **fact** or O if it is an **opinion**.

_____ Students should use mnemonics more often to memorize information and to study for tests

Lesson #25

1. Which two movie categories make up one-half of the pie chart?

   Musicals and Animated
   Comedy and Action
   Other and Action
   Action and Animated
   Super Heroes and Animated
   Sci-Fi and Animated

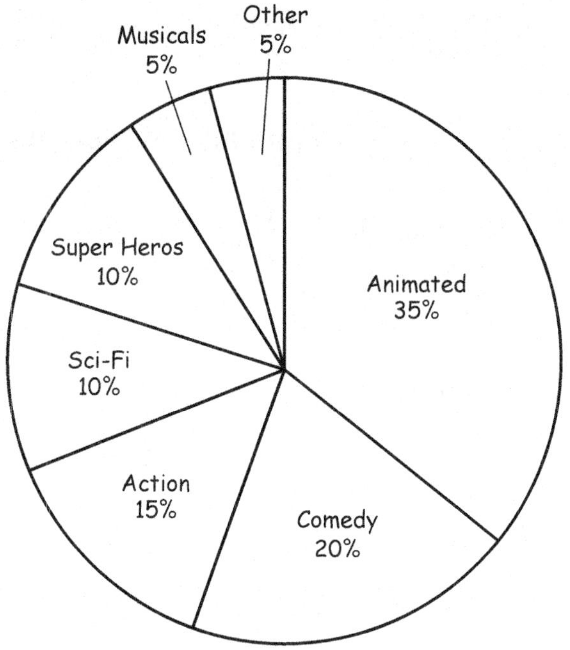

Favorite Movie Categories

2. What information is missing from the graph?

   A) No information is missing.
   B) the title and labels of categories
   C) information about whose favorites are shown
   D) the percentage for category

3. Which is the best resource for finding out which films received Academy Awards in 2010?

   atlas thesaurus dictionary almanac

4. Which of these are reasons for using a bibliography? Check all that apply.

   _____ to avoid plagiarism
   _____ to make a report more legible
   _____ to make a report seem longer
   _____ to list sources of information
   _____ to give other authors credit for their work

5. Read all of the sentences in the paragraph and decide which one is the topic sentence. Then draw a line under the topic sentence.

The baseball cap is a practical and well-liked part of the player's uniform. It has been around a long time — over 150 years, in fact. Members of the Brooklyn Excelsiors first wore baseball caps in 1860, and today, you can find them in just about any country. The brim of the cap was designed to keep the sun out of the players' eyes, which makes the cap practical. However, many non-baseball players wear the caps because they are stylish as well as sensible.

6 – 8. Write the letter of the best resource for locating each of the following items. Use each choice only once.

A) almanac	C) dictionary	E) thesaurus
B) atlas	D) encyclopedia	F) Internet

_______ an alphabetical listing of synonyms and antonyms

_______ maps showing continents, countries, oceans, and land features

_______ an electronic network of computers; all types of resources can be found there

_______ fast facts, lists, or information such as the Nobel Peace prize winners during the last half of the 20th century

_______ an alphabetical listing of words, pronunciations, parts of speech, and definitions

_______ an information bank containing articles on a variety of topics and written by experts

Lesson #26

Read the paragraph; then complete the items that follow.

It took humans thousands of years to advance from hand tools to the invention of machines. Just think of how many **innovative** creations have been developed in the last 100 years! Humans have witnessed the development of cars, radio, television, airplanes, spaceships, computers, air conditioning, highways, and lasers. Technology is growing faster today than ever before in history.

1. Underline the sentence that states the main idea of the paragraph.

2. Use context clues in the paragraph to select an antonym for *innovative*.

   original commonplace creative new

3. 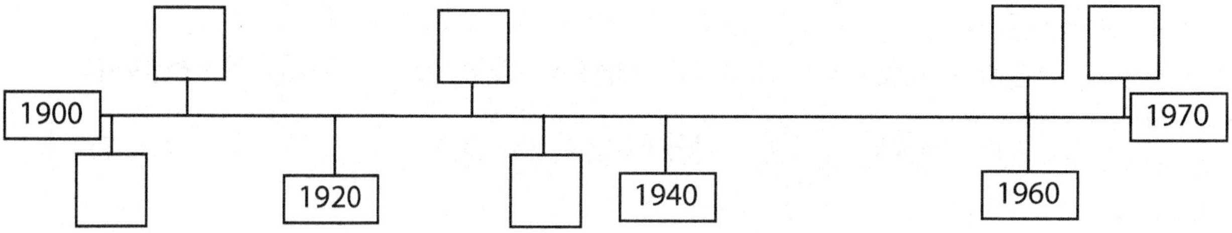

   Place the letter of each event in its proper place on the timeline.

   A) the Internet, 1969
   B) laser, 1960
   C) air flight, 1903
   D) air conditioning, 1911
   E) FM radio, 1933
   F) Television, 1927

4. Which of these is the best acrostic to use if you want to remember the first five United States presidents in order? (Washington, Adams, Jefferson, Madison, and Monroe)

   A) All jackhammers make wonderful music.
   B) Wash and mend jumpers methodically.
   C) Watermelon and jellybeans mix marvelously!
   D) Molly and Michael work joyfully

Read the following three-point essay item.

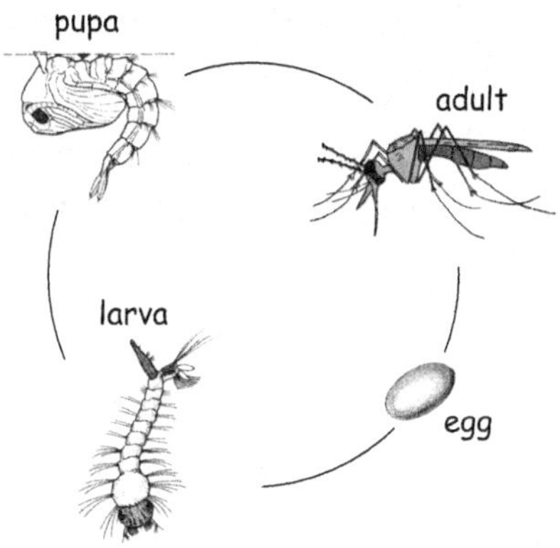

List the four stages of complete metamorphosis. Give one example of an organism that goes through complete metamorphosis. Draw a diagram showing the four stages.

5. What does the essay prompt ask the test taker to do? Check all that apply.

_____ draw a diagram

_____ write a definition

_____ list four stages of metamorphosis

_____ create a chart

_____ give an example

6. Which of these would be the best way to begin a response to the essay item?

A) Organisms are living things and they lay eggs that grow into adults.

B) Either a housefly or a butterfly; they are both insects.

C) The four stages of complete metamorphosis are egg, pupa, larva, and adult.

D) A diagram would be sort of like a circle with pictures of an adult fly and all the other stages.

Write C if the underlined part states a **cause** or E if it states an **effect**.

7. _____ <u>A special license is required of anyone who works as an accountant at the firm</u>, so Philip signed up for a certification program at a local college.

8. _____ <u>The accounting firm has an excellent reputation</u> because of its outstanding customer service, top-notch employees, and technical expertise.

Lesson #27

1. Between which two months did the sharpest decline in average temperatures occur?

____

____

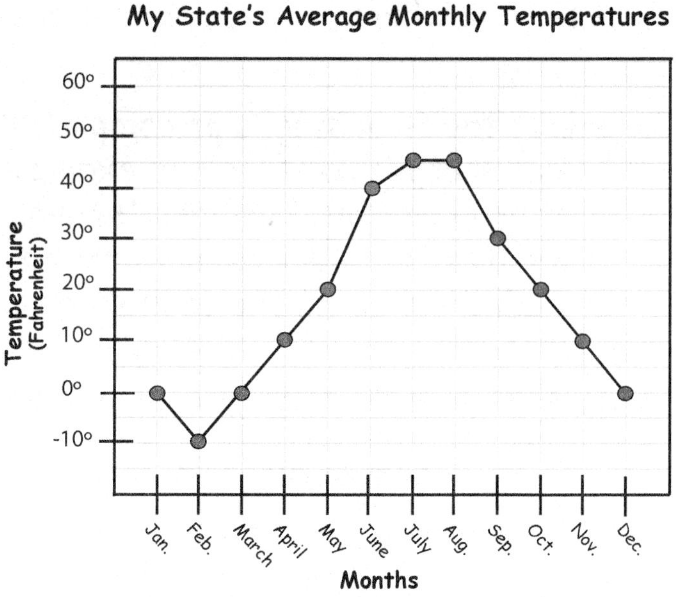

2. Based on the data in the graph, which state do you think the graph is about?

Florida Hawaii Alaska Tennessee

3. Find and read the "Test-Taking Strategies" section of the *Help Pages* on page 69. Then complete each sentence by filling in the blanks.

Test-Taking Strategies

Before you begin, listen carefully, and read every word of the test ______________________________. Write your answers ____________________________. Complete every item, even if you have to make a ______________________________. Go back over your work once you have ______________________________ the test.

Study Strategy Time management is important when you are taking a test. Be aware of how much time is allowed and how much time you should spend on each question. Wear a watch if you are not able to see a clock from your seat. And be sure to allow time to check your answers.

4. Which of these are ways to avoid plagiarism? Check all that apply.

____ use several sources

____ paraphrase what you have learned

____ use your own words

____ include a bibliography or give credit to the original authors

5. Which are the **two** best resources for finding a list of all the cities that have hosted the Winter Olympics?

almanac   thesaurus   Internet website   none of these

6. Choose the word pair that best completes the analogy.

police force : chief :: ____________________

school : principal   driver : highway patrol

airplane : engine   studio : dance instructor

Write F for **fact**, O for **opinion**, or B for **both**.

7. _____ Dictatorship is one form of government, and both Cuba and North Korea are countries that are run by dictatorships.

8. _____ Democracy is defined as "rule by the people"; it is the most acceptable type of government.

Lesson #28

Why a Round Table?

Folklore has it that during the reign of King Arthur, a large round table was specifically designed to prevent jealousy and envy among the noblemen. The legendary Middle Ages British ruler decided to put an end to constant bickering and positioning for power at the head of the long table. The problem was solved when the king seated his warriors at a circular table — in equal positions, where no one was made to feel more or less important. King Arthur emphasized a "code of **chivalry**," and he expected the knights at the table to follow the code. The code required them to be courteous, loyal, and sociable.

1. Which of these best summarizes the main idea of the paragraph?

   A) King Arthur was a famous ruler during the Middle Ages.
   B) The idea of a "round table" came from King Arthur during the Middle Ages.
   C) Before the time of King Arthur, warriors tended to be jealous and uncivil toward each other.
   D) King Arthur was a genius and an excellent emperor.

2. Use context clues: **chivalry** means about the same as ___________.

   dictatorship   wealthy class   politeness   power struggle

3. **Folklore** means about the same as ________.

   legend   warriors   olden times   furniture

4. Which **two** resources would be best for finding more information about the Knights of the Round Table?

   ◯ dictionary   ◯ atlas
   ◯ almanac   ◯ the Internet
   ◯ encyclopedia   ◯ thesaurus

Use information from the schedule to complete items 5–7.

TECHNOBOTS Morning Camp Schedule

	Monday	Tuesday	Wednesday	Thursday	Friday
8:00 – 9:00	Breakfast and Tent Cleanup				
9:00 – 10:00	Lego Robots	Lego Robots	Lego Robots	Lego Robots	Lego Robots (Competition)
10:00 – 11:00	Edible Science Experience	CSI: Finger-prints	Edible Science Experience	CSI: Finger-prints	Edible Science Experience
11:00 – 12:00	What Makes It Tick?	What Makes It Tick?	What Makes It Tick?	Nature Hike	Techno Arts & Crafts
Noon	Lunch				

5. On which days will the TECHNOBOTS learn to make science experiments that they can eat?

Monday Tuesday Wednesday Thursday Friday

6. When does the nature hike take place?

____

7. Which events happen every day of the week?

A) Lego activities, nature hike, and arts & crafts
B) Science experiments, robots, and cleanup
C) tent cleanup, lunch, and Lego activities
D) breakfast, fingerprinting, and science experiments

8. Choose the word that best completes the analogy.

chivalry : graciousness :: plagiarism : ____________

studious stealing mannerly intelligence

Lesson #29

The chart below lists facts about two famous sled dogs, Balto and Togo. Both are remembered as "dog heroes" who had a mission to travel across the icy and brutally cold Alaskan tundra. During a diphtheria epidemic in a remote part of Alaska, mushers and their dog teams, led by Balto and Togo, brought an important serum that saved the lives of many people. The **serum** run began in Nenana, Alaska and ended in Nome, Alaska.

1. According to the context clues, what does a *serum* do?

   keeps people warm   moves across ice   fights an illness

Two Famous Sled Dogs

Balto	Both	Togo
• Lifespan: 1919–1933 • Musher: Gunnar Kaasen • Retirement: Ohio • Taxidermied: Cleveland Natural History Museum • Finished the serum run in Nome • Most famous sled dog (1995 animated film; statue is in Central Park, NY)	• Siberian Husky • Member of the Great Race of Mercy in 1925 • Statue is in Cleveland Metroparks Zoo • Faced blizzard conditions, -23°F, severe winds • Remembered annually during Iditarod	• Lifespan: 1913–1929 • Musher: Leonhard Seppala • Retirement: Maine • Taxidermied and on display at Iditarod Headquarters in Wasilla, Alaska • Began the serum run out of Nenana • Less notoriety than Balto

2. Study the chart and use the information to complete items 2–7.

   A) What other graphic organizer would be best for showing the information in the three-column chart?

   timeline   pie graph   line graph   Venn diagram

   B) According to the three-column chart, which sled dog first led the serum run that began in Nenana, Alaska?

   Balto   Togo   Both

3. Taxidermy is a process used to mount animals for display using their actual skin and fur. Which Siberian Husky is on display at the Iditarod Headquarters in Wasilla, Alaska?

   Balto Togo Both

4. Which dog's life was featured in an animated film?

   Balto Togo Both

5. Rank these topics in order from general to specific. The most general is number one.

   _____ dog _____ Balto _____ mammal

   __1__ vertebrate _____ sled dog _____ Siberian husky

Write F for **fact**, O for opinion, or B for **both**.

6. _____ Togo was an even greater hero than Balto because Togo led the first part of the journey, and he traveled farther.

7. _____ In 1925, at least five children in Nome died of diphtheria before the teams were able to deliver the serum.

Read the sentence below. Does the underlined part tell the cause or the effect?

8. Today, <u>diphtheria is controlled</u> because children are given a vaccine against the disease.

   cause effect neither

Siberian Husky

Lesson #30

Flo's Flooded Basement on Saturation Street

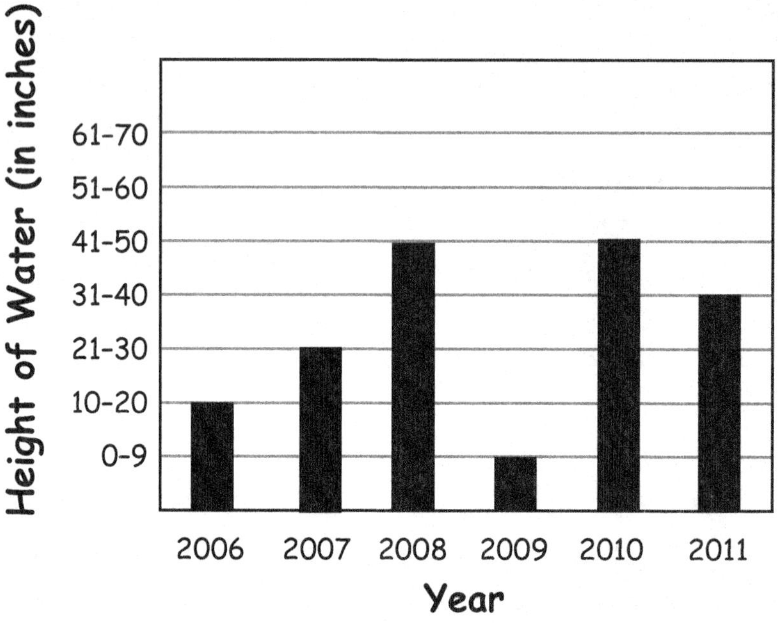

1. During which year(s) did Flo have about 4 feet of water in her basement?

   2006 2007 2008 2009 2010 2011

2. Severe thunderstorms cause basement flooding on Saturation Street. Which year was probably the driest, based on information in the graph?

   2006 2007 2008 2009 2010 2011

3. Exactly how much water did Flo have in her basement in 2007?

   21 inches 25 inches

   30 inches information not given

4. Choose the word that best completes the analogy.

   ignorant : uninformed :: _________ : well-informed

   unaware knowledgeable naïve lacking

When an organism feeds on the blood of another organism, this is called hematophagy. Bedbugs are one of the world's most effective hematophages. A bedbug can drink 7 times its own body weight in blood. By comparison, a mosquito only drinks 1.5 times its weight in blood.

5. Underline the part that gives a definition for *hematophagy.*

6. Why are bedbugs an example of *hematophagous* animals?

A) They are a current problem all over the world.
B) They feed on human blood.
C) They are bigger than mosquitoes.
D) They are invisible.

7. The context clues let you know that the Greek root *hema* probably means "_______________."

bug organism feed blood

Comparison of Two Flying Animals

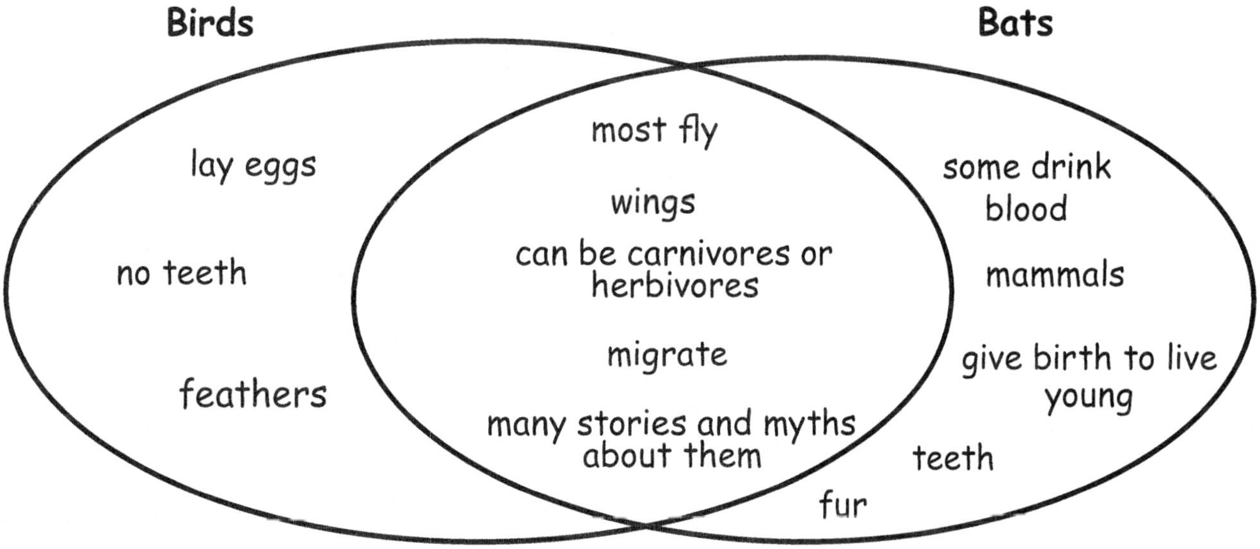

8. Which animal moves from one habitat to another in search of food or seasonal shelter?

bat bird both neither

Summer Solutions.

Minutes a Day-Mastery for a Lifetime!

Level 5

Study Skills

Help Pages

Help Pages

Glossary	
acronym	*see* example on page 78
acrostic	*see* example on page 78
almanac	a reference book that is a single volume of current facts, figures, tables, and lists
antonym	a word that means the opposite of another word
antonym analogy	compares two sets of words or objects that are opposites; for example, light : dark :: open : shut
atlas	a reference book that is a collection of maps
bar graph	a graph that uses bars to compare data or information
bibliography	an alphabetical listing (by author's last name) of sources used to prepare and write a report or other paper
category	a grouping of things that are alike
chart	used to organize a large amount of information
chronological	numerical order; first, second, third, and so on
column graph	a graph that uses vertical bars to compare data or information
circle graph	*see* **pie graph**
completion item	*see* **fill-in item**
context clues	word clues that give the meaning of a word in the same or a nearby sentence; clues can be synonyms, antonyms, or definitions
data	information such as facts, numbers, or measurements
definition context clue	two or more words in a nearby sentence that give the definition of the word
description context clue	describing words in a nearby sentence to help give the meaning of the word
diagram	a drawing used to illustrate a concept

Help Pages

Glossary	
dictionary	a reference book in which words are listed in alphabetical order; also gives pronunciation, definition, and other information
direction word	a word that tells what to do; Examples: *compare, define, describe, list, explain, summarize*
encyclopedia	a reference book that contains articles on many topics; listed in alphabetical order
essay question	a question or statement that calls for an extended response (4–5 sentences); the response should be written in paragraph form
fill-in item	an item that calls for the student to fill in a missing word or words
flash cards	cards that are used to help memorize information
glossary	an alphabetical listing of words and their meanings; usually found at the back of a book
grouping	putting things in lists or categories to assist in memorizing
horizontal	flat or level 
index	an alphabetical listing found at the back of a book; includes important terms, names, and illustrations found in the book, page numbers
Internet	a vast network of digital information that can be accessed by computers
key	tells what the symbol on a graph or map stands for; also known as a legend;
line graph	a graph that uses dots and lines to compare information over a period of time
main idea	what a paragraph or selection is about
matching item	an item that requires putting like things together; for example, a word and its definition

Help Pages

Glossary	
mnemonic device	a strategy for remembering; examples of mnemonics include acronym words and sentences or rhyming
paraphrase	to put something in your own words
pictograph	a chart that uses pictures or symbols to show information
pie graph	also known as a pie chart or circle graph; it is divided into pie-shaped pieces, each slice representing some information that is part of the whole
plagiarism	the illegal use of another person's words or ideas
prefix	parts added to the beginning of a word that change the meaning of the word
resource	source of information; for example, dictionary, encyclopedia, thesaurus, Internet, almanac, atlas, etc.
rhyming	putting together words with similar endings, such as *right - tight - might*; may be used to learn or memorize information
root word	the main part of a word; stands on its own without a prefix or suffix
search engine	a computer program that searches for different websites to locate information
source	a starting place; where information comes from; for example, book, encyclopedia, website, interview (*see* **resource**)
strategy	a plan for solving a problem or doing a task
suffix	parts added to the end of a word that change the meaning of the word
summarize	to restate only the main points or ideas in a selection using your own words

Help Pages

Glossary	
supporting details	information that adds to the main idea or topic sentence
synonym	a word that means the same or nearly the same as another word
synonym analogy	compares two sets of words or objects that are alike in some way; for example, *happy : glad :: big : large*
synonym context clue	a word clue that is a synonym for another word within a passage
table	used to organize a large amount of information
table of contents	an outline located near the front of a book; lists chapter titles (or major topics) and page numbers
thesaurus	a reference book that gives synonyms, and sometimes antonyms, of words
timeline	a way to organize events and dates; timelines can be horizontal or vertical
topic sentence	sentence that contains the main idea; may come at the beginning, middle, or end of a paragraph
true or false item	a statement that is either true or not true; if any part is false, the statement is false
Venn diagram	a chart used to compare and contrast information (shows similarities and differences)
vertical	up and down ↕
visual clues	illustrations, photos, or graphics that give clues about the meaning of what is written
website	a place on the Internet that contains information in the form of pictures, text, videos, and sound
World Wide Web	a part of the Internet; sometimes used interchangeably with the word *Internet*

Help Pages

Summary of Study Strategies and Suggestions

Develop and use good listening skills.

Keep an assignment notebook or folder.

Have the right supplies.

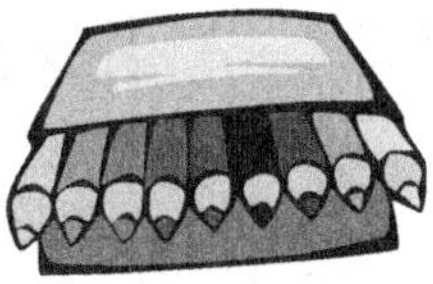

Read as much as you can.

Organize storage areas.

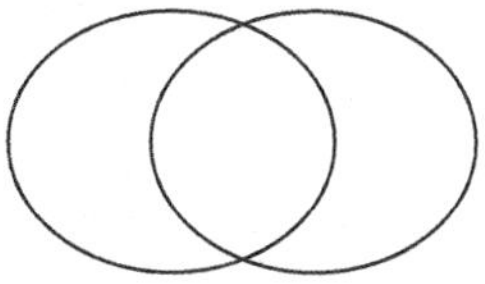

Use graphic organizers to summarize information.

Set goals.

Have a study buddy.

Get plenty of sleep and eat a nutritional breakfast.

Manage your time; don't wait until the last minute to complete assignments or study for a test.

Visit museums, zoos, aquariums, and other educational places that are also fun.

Use special strategies to help you memorize.

- Break up large amounts of information into chunks.
- Use rhyming, flashcards, and acronyms.

FYI

Help Pages

Summary of Test-Taking Strategies and Suggestions

Listen carefully to all directions.

Read every word of the test directions.

Underline key words in the directions.

Read each test question or statement carefully.

Brainstorm ideas for essay items and organize your ideas before you start writing (Use scrap paper.)

fish breathe with gills

Write your answers neatly.

Know how much time you have and manage your time. (Do not spend too much time on any one item.)

If there are multiple choices, if permitted, cross out any answers that are definitely wrong

~~A~~ ~~B~~ C D

Complete every item, even if you have to make a guess.

Go back over your work once you have finished the test.

Change an answer only if you are sure you have answered incorrectly.

Help Pages

Graphic Organizers

Inverted Pyramid

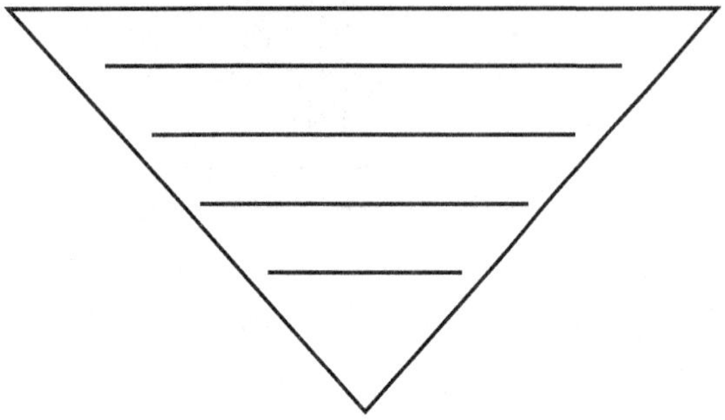

Venn Diagram

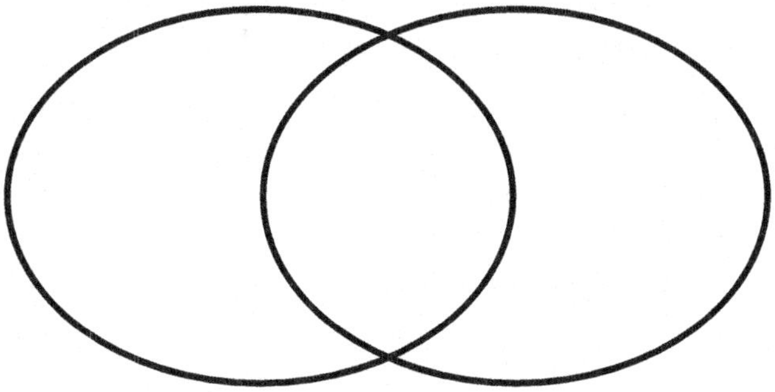

Table

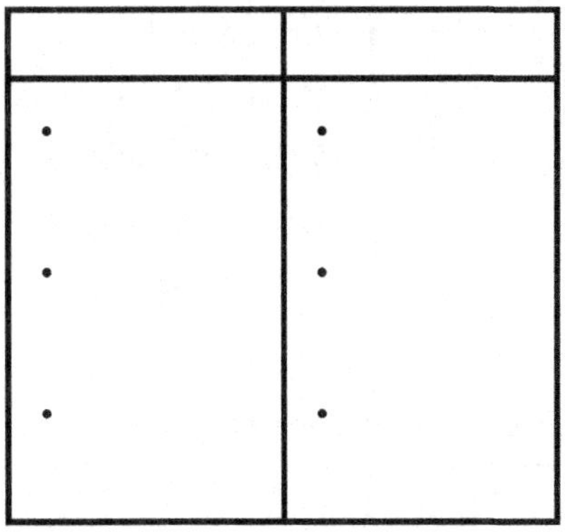

Chart

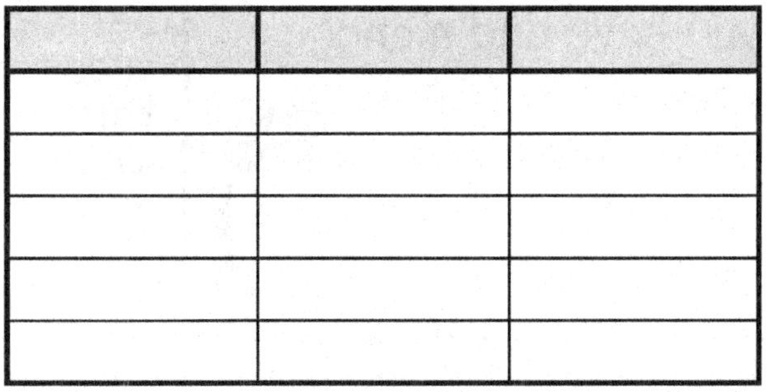

Web

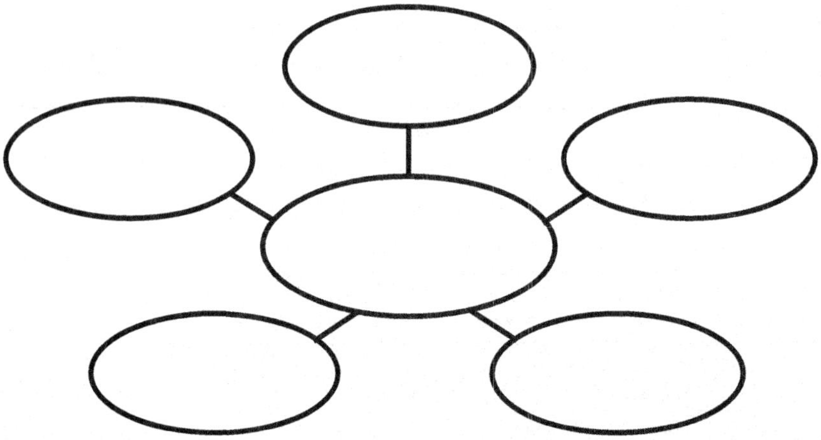

Help Pages

References		
	**almanac**	a book of current facts, published every year; contains facts, figures, tables, and lists
	**atlas**	a collection of maps showing continents, countries, oceans, and physical land features
	**dictionary**	an alphabetical listing of words and their meanings; entries include pronunciation, part of speech, and word origin
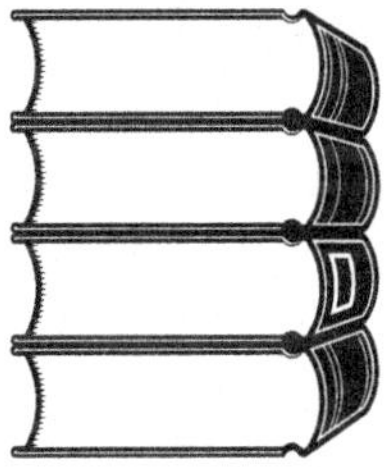	**encyclopedia**	an information bank; contains articles written by experts and arranged in alphabetical order; articles cover many topics
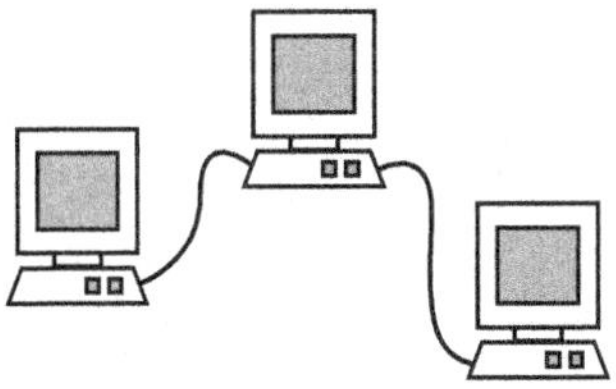	**Internet**	an electronic network connecting computers all over the world; often used interchangeably with World Wide Web
	**thesaurus**	an alphabetical listing of synonyms and antonyms; used to find substitute words and to build vocabulary

Help Pages

Bibliography
A bibliography is a list of sources that were used in the preparation of a research document. The bibliography is arranged in alphabetical order by author's name. The title of the book, magazine, or Internet article is included, as well as the publisher, date of publication, and sometimes page numbers. Bibliography styles may differ slightly, and you should follow your teacher's specific directions for setting up your bibliography. Here are some guidelines and examples of how to list various sources. The following use MLA format. **Some of the information listed here may not be available. If the information is not available, just include as much as you can find in the citation.**
Book with One Author: Author's Last name, First name. Title of Book. City: Publisher, Date. **Example:** Lawry, Matthew. Fascinating Desert Life Forms. Dayton: Traders Press, 2004.
Book with Two or Three Authors: Author's Last name, First name and additional author's First and Last name(s). Title of Book. City: Publisher, Date. **Example:** Morris, Paul, Trudy Willis, and Marie Jenson. Hiker Meets Cactus. Chicago: Toads Press, 2008.
Encyclopedia: Author's Last name, First name (if available). "Title of Article." Title of Encyclopedia. City: Publisher, year ed. **Example:** Hernandez, Noreen. "Arid Biomes." Universe Encyclopedia. New York: Green, Inc., 2006 ed.

Help Pages

Bibliography (continued)

Magazine Article:

Author's Last name, First name. "Article Title." Title of Magazine Month year: page numbers.

Example:

Parched, Sandy. "My Days in the Sahara." Geography and More May 2000: 13-19.

Internet Article:

Author's Last name, First name. "Article Title." Website Title. Date of posting or last update. Site sponsor. Date you visited the website. <web address>.

Example:

Greenberg, Tasha. "Desert Life." Topics to Research. March 2006. International Geographics. Sept. 16, 2010. <http://topicstoresearch.com/biomes/desert.html>.

Website with No Author:

"Site Title." Sponsor. Copyright date or latest update. Date you visited the website. <web address>.

Example:

"Desert Days." Environments Global. 2009. Aug. 23, 2010. <http://environsglobal.net/days/desert.html>.

Personal Interview:

Person's Last name, First name. Kind of interview (personal interview or phone call). Date of interview.

Example:

Jogan, James. Personal interview. February 20, 2007.

Help Pages

Test-Taking Strategies

Doing well on tests is a great goal, and there are many strategies to help you to do better. A **strategy** is a tactic or a plan. The best plan is simply to know the material. If you have paid attention in class, done your homework, and asked for help when you needed it, you are probably well-prepared to take a test. Knowing the facts that you will be tested on will give you **confidence**. And, when you believe in yourself, you usually do better!

Follow these three steps when taking any type of test:

Step 1: Listen carefully to the person giving the test. If you are unsure about anything, ask questions before the test begins.

Step 2: Carefully read EVERY word in the directions. This will help you to know exactly what you are expected to do.

Step 3: Look for key words in the directions and test items. If you are allowed to write on the test, highlight, underline, or circle the key words. Here are some examples of key words: *check, circle, classify, describe, number, select, underline*, and *write.*

Help Pages

Test-Taking Strategies (continued)

Multiple Choice

A multiple-choice test has questions with several answer choices. The test taker must choose the correct answer. Usually, only one answer choice is correct. These suggestions may help you to improve your score on multiple-choice tests.

- Read the directions carefully. Do the directions say to circle, fill in, or underline? Do the directions tell you to choose **one** answer or select **all** that apply?
- Read all choices before you choose your answer. If allowed, put a tiny x next to the choices that are definitely NOT correct.
- Watch for words like *always, all,* or *never.* These words are often found in wrong answers.
- If an answer does not make sense, it is usually wrong.
- If two of the choices are opposites, one is usually the right answer.
- Answer every question even if you have to guess. Do not leave blanks.

Help Pages

Test-Taking Strategies (continued)

True or False

Even though your chance of correctly answering a true or false test item is 50/50, this type of test can be very tricky. Study the following strategies to help improve your odds.

- Read the entire statement before answering. If any part of the statement is false, then the answer is <u>false</u>.
- Words like *not,* or prefixes such as *un-* or *dis-*, can change the meaning of the entire statement.
- Watch out for words like *all, no, every, only, never,* and *always.* These words usually make a statement <u>false</u>.
- Words like *some, many, usually, most,* and *sometimes* are often found in <u>true</u> statements.
- The word *because* sometimes makes the statement <u>false</u>.

Help Pages

Test-Taking Strategies (continued)

Completion or Fill-in

A **completion** or **fill-in** question contains an item with a blank space. Part of the statement is missing. You must write an answer in the blank space. Here are some tips for taking a fill-in test:

- Listen to the teacher's instructions carefully. Find out if the size of the blank is related to the length of the answer. Is there only one word per blank?
- Write or print very clearly. If your answer is not clear, it may be marked wrong.
- Look for hints, such as spelling, in other items.
- If you are not sure of an answer, take an educated guess! You may get partial credit.
- Finally, read the whole statement with your answer included. It should make sense and sound right. If it does not, your answer is probably incorrect.

Read these sample test items. The answers are in parentheses.

1. ____________________ (Digestion) is the process in which food is broken down, so the body can absorb and use it.
2. Digestion begins in the ____________________ (mouth) when you chew and swallow.
3. The __________________________ (esophagus) is a food canal that leads to the ___________________ (stomach) where food is temporarily stored and mixed up with liquids and digestive juices.

Notice the clues.

- The answer to item 1 is actually given and spelled correctly in item 2.
- Context clues "chew and swallow" let you know that the answer to item 2 is "mouth."

Help Pages

How to Write an Acronym

An **acronym** is a word that is formed from the first initials of the items that need to be memorized. **Example**: BLT for "bacon, lettuce, and tomato"

Step 1: List the items that you need to memorize.

Step 2: Underline the first letter of each item.

Step 3: Arrange the underlined letters to form a real word or a nonsense word. Here are some examples:

- Nonsense word: **NASA** (an acronym for National Aeronautics and Space Administration)
- Real word: **HOMES** (stands for the names of the Great Lakes (Huron, Ontario, Michigan, Erie, and Superior).

How to Write an Acrostic

An **acrostic** is a sentence in which the beginning letters of each word match the letters of an item to be remembered. For example, "Any skunk is a pest" for names of the five oceans (Arctic, Southern, Indian, Atlantic, Pacific)

Step 1: List the items that you need to memorize.

Step 2: Underline the first letter of each item.

Step 3: Arrange the underlined letters to form a sentence that is easy to remember.

Here are some examples:

- My Very Educated Mother Just Served Us Nachos. This helps you to remember the names of the planets in order from the sun: Mercury, Venus, Earth, Mars, Jupiter, Saturn, Uranus, and Neptune.
- Eat An Apple As A Nighttime Snack. These beginning letters can help you to remember the names of the seven continents: Europe, Antarctica, Africa, Asia, Australia, North America, and South America.

Help Pages

Cause and Effect

An **effect** tells <u>what</u> happened. The **cause** tells <u>why</u> it happened.

Example: Cause: There was a blizzard overnight,
Effect: and the roads are closed today.

Ask yourself, "What happened?" The roads are closed. (Effect)
Ask yourself, "Why did it happen?" There was a blizzard overnight. (Cause)

A cause may have more than one effect.

Example: Cause: There was a blizzard overnight,
Effects: so the roads are closed today and snow plows have to work overtime.

An effect may be the cause of something else.

Example: Cause: The roads are closed today;
Effect: therefore school is cancelled.
Cause: Since school is canceled,
Effect: we are taking our sleds to the park.

blizzard ➔ roads closed ➔ schools canceled ➔ sled rides in the park

Sometimes special clue words and phrases can signal a cause or effect.

as a result of	consequently	hence	so	thus
because	due to	since	therefore	

Remember, the <u>order</u> of cause and effect statements can change. Either can come first in a sentence.

Example: Cause: The oven got too hot,
Effect: so the cookies burned.
Effect: The cookies burned
Cause: because the oven got too hot.

Help Pages

Context Clues

You can use **context clues** to figure out the meaning of a word. Context clues are the words that come before or after the unknown word.

Sometimes the author will give the definition of the new word by using **synonyms**.

Example 1: The farmers get fair **remuneration**, or payment, for the goods they provide.

The context clues let you know that *remuneration* must mean *payment.*

Example 2: Margo's biggest **gaffe** was that she called the teacher by her first name. That was a mistake!

You can tell that *gaffe* means *mistake.* The next sentence says exactly that. Also, you probably know that calling a teacher by her first name would be a mistake.

Sometimes the author will hint about the meaning of the word by using antonyms.

Example 1: Claire was actually **garrulous** this morning. Usually she barely speaks.

The context clues let you know that *garrulous* must mean the opposite of *barely speaks.* So, *garrulous* must mean *talkative.*

Example 2: When the teacher was gone during recess, the kindergarten room was **chaotic**! I longed for my own peaceful, quiet classroom.

You can tell that *chaotic* means the opposite of *peaceful* and *quiet.* Also, you can imagine recess in a room full of five-year-olds without their teacher.

Help Pages

Context Clues (continued)

If you cannot figure out the meaning of a word, it's a good idea to first decide what part of speech the word is.

Example: Dr. Foster had photos of beautiful **tetras** in his office.

Which of these tells the meaning of *tetras*?

acrobats cooking fish jumps

This sentence doesn't tell you what *tetras* are, but you can tell that *tetra* is a **plural noun**. So it is probably not *cooking* or *jumps*.

Read the next part: Tetras are so brightly colored! Imagine seeing them swimming in large schools in the clear rivers of South America.

Which of these tells the meaning of *tetras*?

acrobats ~~cooking~~ fish ~~jumps~~

The context clues — *swimming in large schools in the clear rivers of South America* — tell you that *tetras* must be a *type of colorful fish*.

Help Pages

Analogies

An **analogy** is a way of comparing things.

Here is an example: mayor : city :: governor : state

You say,

"Mayor is to city as governor is to state."

To solve an analogy, you need to figure out what the relationship is between the two words.

A *mayor* is the leader of a city. A *governor* is the leader of a state.

Here is another example: lamb : sheep :: calf : ________

What is the relationship? A lamb is a baby sheep.

horse piglet cow kitten

The missing word must be *cow* because a *calf* is a baby *cow.*

In an **analogy**, the words may be compared in many ways.

The words may be synonyms.

Example: happy : joyful :: tall : high

Happy and *joyful* are synonyms. *Tall* and *high* are synonyms.

The words may be antonyms.

Example: thin : thick :: rich : poor

Thin is the opposite of *thick.* *Rich* is the opposite of *poor.*

One word may describe the other.

Example: bright : sunshine :: prickly : porcupine

Sunshine is *bright.* A *porcupine* is *prickly.*

One word may name a part of the other.

Example: wheels : bicycle :: legs : table

A *bicycle* has *wheels.* A *table* has *legs.*

One word may be in the category or group of the other.

Example: rabbit : mammal :: orange : fruit

A *rabbit* is a type of *mammal.* An *orange* is a type of *fruit.*

Summer Solutions.

Minutes a Day-Mastery for a Lifetime!

Level 5

Study Skills

Answers to Lessons

Lesson #1		Lesson #2		Lesson #3	
1	The **main idea** is what a selection is mostly about.	1	B	1	summarize
2	"What is this writing mostly about?"	2	vegetable	2	The Spanish people had many reasons for coming to North America.
3	one	3	helicopter	3	✓search for riches ✓convert the people ✓colonize the New World
4	C	4	prickly	4	● Why the Spanish Came...
5	walking riding on horseback horse-drawn wagons boats	5	clever	5	conquerors
6	dangerous hazardous	6	● A subterranean river is...	6	middle
7	D	7	C	7	2 1 5 3 4
8	A	8	main idea	8	main idea

Lesson #4		Lesson #5		Lesson #6	
1	A	1 - 2	A B	1	The invention of Velcro was the direct result of an encounter with Mother Nature.
2	words			2	● Although de Mestral's...
3	A	3	Because of the November election, a new mayor will preside...	3	D
4	D	4	The new mayor is in favor of recycling; hence, a curbside recycling program...	4	B
5	C	5	jarring sound	5	common
6	D	6	accidental and lucky	6	C
7	"What is this writing mostly about?"	7	both of these	7	E
8	piano	8	thesaurus	8	A) Inventors B) Swiss Inventors C) George de Mestral

Lesson #7		Lesson #8		Lesson #9	
1	F	1	A **mnemonic** (ni•**mon**•ik) is a memory strategy. An **acronym** is a word that is made from the first initials of the words you need to remember.	1	rhyming
2	O	2	PALE	2	visualization
3	F	3	HOMES	3	flashcards
4	West Virginia is an excellent place for hiking	4	PEN	4	● Very many cute...
5	...is most vibrant and beautiful during the peak of autumn.	5	NEWS	5	all of these
6	this magnificent tree was the most...	6	C B A	6	● Chrissy, my other cat...
7	order	7	F	7	both
8	make known	8	O	8	descend

Lesson #10		Lesson #11		Lesson #12	
1	The Japanese people have beautiful traditions for remembering their loved ones who have died.	1	solar power	1	Comparing Alligators and Crocodiles
2	C	2	small bedroom	2	Crocodiles
3	A) ancestors B) decorated	3	June 2011	3	Alligators
4	~~tradition~~	4	B	4	11
5	● When you are drinking...	5	November year	5	8
6	rhyming	6	O	6	3
7	main idea	7	B	7	E
8	a cause an effect	8	F	8	C

Lesson #13		Lesson #14		Lesson #15	
1	High Points in Alaska's History	1	B	1	At least half the people in Berryton speak English.
2	4 5 2 1 3	2	Yosemite Mount Rushmore Yellowstone Lincoln Memorial	2	100%
3	Russia	3	Petrified Forest	3	C
4	gold	4	D	4	D
5	chronological	5	B	5	15 million pounds
6	FRAMB	6	A	6	name of the country exporting corn
7	Venn diagram	7	B	7	D
8	F F	8	B	8	line graph — shows trends or change... bar or pictograph — compares the data ... pie or circle graph — shows parts of a whale

Lesson #16

1	tusks
2	ears
3	3 3
4	D
5	farming
6	200,000 acres
7	wheat
8	160 days

Lesson #17

1	• mammals • herbivores • live in herds • females are called cows • males are called bulls • like to be near water • have trunks
2	• larger • have bigger ears • cows and bulls have tusks • round smooth heads • trunks have two-finger-like extensions • may live for 70 years • threatened species
3	• smaller • smaller, more rounded ears • heads have two humps • males have visible tusks • trunks only have one finger-like extension • live for a period up to 60 years • highly endangered species
4 - 8	See table below

African Elephant	Both	Asian Elephant
See #2 Above	See #1 Above	See #3 Above

Lesson #18

1 - 4 (matching):

If any part of a true or false statement is false,	the entire statement is false.
After you have looked over a test,	begin by doing the easiest items first.
Before the test begins, make sure	you know how many minutes you have, so you can manage your time.
Complete every item on the test	even if you have to make a guess.

5	D
6	6
7	8
8	2

<table>
<tr><th colspan="2">Lesson #19</th><th colspan="2">Lesson #20</th><th colspan="2">Lesson #21</th></tr>
<tr><td>1</td><td>✓describe... ✓name...</td><td>1</td><td>B</td><td rowspan="3">1 - 3</td><td rowspan="3">Internet
almanac
thesaurus
atlas
dictionary
encyclopedia</td></tr>
<tr><td>2</td><td>C</td><td>2</td><td>instinct</td></tr>
<tr><td>3</td><td>Summarize
explain</td><td>3</td><td>stalk</td></tr>
<tr><td>4</td><td>Henry Ford became the greatest genius of the twentieth century...</td><td>4</td><td>tame</td><td>4</td><td>main idea</td></tr>
<tr><td>5</td><td>...beyond what anyone could have imagined.</td><td>5</td><td>annoying</td><td>5</td><td>pie graph</td></tr>
<tr><td>6</td><td>Everyone should know that...</td><td rowspan="3">6 - 8</td><td rowspan="3">table of contents
glossary
captions</td><td>6</td><td>glacier : frozen</td></tr>
<tr><td>7</td><td>E</td><td rowspan="2">7 - 8</td><td rowspan="2">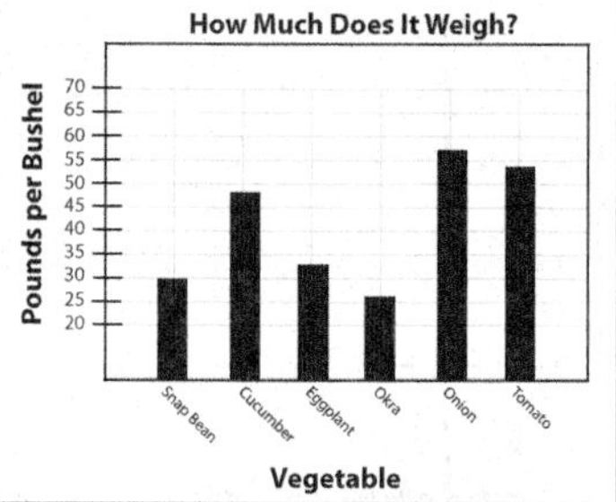
</td></tr>
<tr><td>8</td><td>E</td></tr>
</table>

Lesson #22		Lesson #23		Lesson #24	
1	Plagiarism is the illegal use of another person's words or ideas.	1	Juneau	1	D
2	C	2	2011	2	A) many times bigger B) toxic venomous poison
3	key words	3	A) Diana B) Williams	3	hunter
4	crooked : straight	4	✓ give credit to others ✓ list your sources... ✓ avoid plagiarism	4	massive
5	A) index glossary B) glossary	5	✓ copying and using... ✓ putting your name...	5	violent
6	information several	6	✓summarize and paraphrase, using your own words ✓cite your sources in a bibliography ✓use quotation marks around someone else's actual words	6	victim
7	paraphrase	7	"What is this writing mostly about?"	7	chilly : cold
8	your own words	8	thesaurus	8	O

Lesson #25		Lesson #26		Lesson #27	
1	Action and Animated	1	Technology is growing faster today than ever before in history.	1	August September
2	C	2	commonplace	2	Alaska
3	almanac	3	D F B A C E	3	directions neatly guess finished
4	✓to avoid plagiarism ✓to list sources... ✓to give other authors...	4	C	4	✓use several sources ✓paraphrase what you have learned ✓use your own words ✓include a bibliography or give credit to the original author
5	The baseball cap is a practical and well-liked part of the player's uniform.	5	✓draw a diagram ✓list four stages... ✓give an example	5	almanac Internet website
6 - 8	E B F A C D	6	C	6	school : principal
		7	C	7	F
		8	E	8	B

Lesson #28		Lesson #29		Lesson #30	
1	B	1	fights an illness	1	2008 2010
2	politeness	2	A) Venn diagram B) Togo	2	2009
3	legend	3	Togo	3	information not given
4	● encyclopedia ● the Internet	4	Balto	4	knowledgeable
5	Monday Wednesday Friday	5	vertebrate mammal dog sled dog Siberian Husky Balto	5	When an organism feeds on the blood of another organism, this is called hematophagy.
6	Thursday 11:00	6	B	6	B
7	C	7	F	7	blood
8	stealing	8	effect	8	both